Brussels

Text by Jack Altman and Lindsay Bennett
Updated by George McDonald
Series Editor: Tony Halliday

Berlitz POCKET GUIDE

Brussels

Fourth Edition 2004
Updated 2005

PHOTOGRAPHY
Belgian Tourist Office – Brussels & Wallonia 90; Pete Bennett 6, 13, 15, 19, 22, 26, 28, 31, 33, 34, 37, 38, 41, 43, 45, 47, 49, 50, 52, 55, 56, 61, 83, 84, 92, 93, 95, 102; Chris Coe 58, 97, 105; Jerry Dennis 69, 73, 75, 77; Tony Halliday 16, 70, 71, 72, 76, 78, 86; Erich Lessing/akg-images London 17; Mark Read 9, 21, 40, 88, 100, 101; Georgie Scott 8, 10, 62, 64, 66, 78, 80, 81, 89, 99; George Taylor 23
Front cover: Pete Bennett

CONTACTING THE EDITORS
Every effort has been made to provide accurate information in this publication, but changes are inevitable. The publisher cannot be responsible for any resulting loss, inconvenience or injury. We would appreciate it if readers would call our attention to any errors or outdated information by contacting Berlitz Publishing, PO Box 7910, London SE1 1WE, England. Fax: (44) 20 7403 0290;
e-mail: berlitz@apaguide.co.uk
www.berlitzpublishing.com

The Atomium, a popular symbol of the city, together with buildings from Mini-Europe (page 54)

The Cathédral des Sts-Michel-et-Gudule has many interesting features including the stained-glass in the choir (page 37)

Manneken-Pis, the city's famous statue (page 35)

TOP TEN ATTRACTIONS

The Old England Department Store, one of several impressive Art Nouveau buildings (page 41)

Place Royale, at the heart of Royal Brussels, with the church of St-Jacques-sur-Coudenberg (page 41)

Parc du Cinquantenaire with its monumental arch and museums (page 48)

The Grand-Place, focal point of the city and simply one of the loveliest squares in the world (page 28)

The city of Ghent has numerous attractions, including the picturesque Korenlei (page 82)

Bruges has its canals and the Belfry towering over the Markt (page 70)

Antwerp's Grote Markt has the fountain of the heroic Silvius Brabo (page 62)

CONTENTS

INTRODUCTION

Brussels is the capital of Belgium, a small Western European country of 10 million people set between the Netherlands in the north, France in the south and Germany in the east. When Belgium gained its independence in 1830, Brussels could simply have been content to play its domestic role. Since the end of World War II, however, this city of one million has evolved into an international centre. The headquarters of NATO are here, and the city hosts several key institutions of the European Union (EU), an organisation that has transformed the political and economic climate of the continent. Although Strasbourg and Luxembourg also host EU institutions, no one denies that Brussels is the focal point and heartbeat of the Union. Brussels is an international and cosmopolitan city, where everyone speaks at least two languages, and English speakers have few problems being understood, where the demand for office space is sky-high, and the international airport is one of the fastest-growing in Europe.

Historic Town

One might imagine a 21st-century metropolis of high-rise blocks, with clogged motorways and streets that empty after 5pm. But nothing could be further from the truth. The city's history is a long and rich tapestry dating back many centuries before Belgian independence.

Small by international standards – the city centre can be crossed on foot in about 30 minutes – it is people-friendly. It has a buoyant native population that fills the streets with vibrancy by day and makes it one of the safest of the world's major cities by night. It is a city of delights, and one that has

The town hall on the Grand-Place

the capability to constantly surprise with its architecture, gastronomy and nightlife.

Brussels has been at the heart of European history for much of the last millennium. A trading town on the lucrative route from Eastern Europe to England, it was the leading northern city of the vast Spanish European Empire during the 17th century and of the wealthy Habsburg Austro-Hungarian Empire in the 18th century. However, though Brussels continues to flirt with Europe, it has not yet forgotten that it is first and foremost a Belgian city.

Trading Places

In addition to being a diplomatic centre, it has always been a working and trading town. The pearl that is the old heart of Brussels began its life around the seed of a marketplace in the 14th century. You will discover that many of the street names in the old town hark back to this time, when traders would set up stalls along the narrow, cobbled alleys. Cheese Market, Chicken Market, Grass Market and Butchers' Row – the names conjure up images of bustling medieval Brussels. These same streets still earn their keep, sustaining modern visitors with a wealth of bars and restaurants. The powerful guilds that controlled the skilled trades built large and ornate houses in the centre of town as a visual affirmation of their wealth and influence. They extended a largely benevolent but, when required, brutal control over Brussels' artisans, who were admired around Europe for their skill and workmanship.

European institutions

Théâtre Royal de la Monnaie

On Coudenberg, a hill east of the old town, sat royal and ducal palaces and buildings to house visiting foreign emissaries sent to negotiate with the occupants of the neighbouring palaces.

A dazzling 16th-century town square, the Grand-Place, takes one's breath away with its ornate stonework and gilt decoration. The 14th-century Town Hall is one of the most beautiful examples of civic architecture in Europe. And the narrow streets that surround it are replete with original architectural detail. The skyline on the hill above was transformed during the 18th century in the Louis XVI style, which was *de rigueur* at the time. The palace is still in use by today's Belgian royal family, but it now sits side-by-side with museums dedicated to the arts, filled with collections encompassing the finest Belgian artists and canvasses by a wealth of European masters. In the 19th century, the inspirational King Leopold II gave life to a number of civil construction projects; and in the 20th century, Brussels continued to make architectural history

On parade

with the futuristic Atomium (completed in 1958, just in time for Brussels to host the World's Fair). Almost every corner of the city offers an architectural treat: from Romanesque churches to Gothic towers and Baroque theatres, and a wealth of Art Nouveau – in fact no architecture buff should leave Brussels dissatisfied.

Natives and Foreigners

Thanks to the presence of NATO and the EU, it is said that there are more decision-makers here than in any other city on earth. And yet, when you walk the streets, Brussels does not feel like a powerhouse. It has the gentility and civility of a dowager duchess and it never seems to throw its considerable weight around. Perhaps this is because, even today, the city is not only concerned about world affairs. For every foreign diplomat, there is a shopkeeper, and this 'real activity' helps the city to maintain its pragmatic air.

There is relatively little friction between the natives and the 'army' of foreigners who make Brussels their temporary home. But then this isn't the first foreign 'invasion' to confront the city. The character of the city and its people has been shaped by their country's geography, sandwiched as it has been between two seemingly constantly warring dynasties. Numerous decisive battles have taken place on Belgian soil, Waterloo being but one. Foreigners have usurped this land on many occasions, including both world wars. Today's bloodless diplomatic 'coups' are designed to consign all of this to history.

In the midst of the European détente, Belgium's internal strife may astonish visitors, but with several disparate groups making up the population, differences of opinion on language, education and social services are still being fought out in council chambers and the press. The Flemish north of the country is Dutch-speaking and the Walloon south is French-speaking. There is also a small German-speaking enclave in the east. Brussels caters to both major languages, but beyond the capital you will find that the multilingual signs are less evident.

Despite this domestic friction, the Belgians have a philosophical attitude to life. There's a great deal to like about people who decorate their metro stations with huge canvasses by their best known contemporary artists, and the sides of houses with cartoon or comic strip images. Their natural love of imagery makes Brussels rich in cinema, photography, sculpture and art. With national ballet, opera and theatre companies, there is no shortage of high art, but in addition Brussels embraces with ease novel genres and groundbreaking work.

Underground Art

The Brussels metro provides transport – and more. Art has gone underground, transforming commuter platforms with a wealth of colour and style. All the works on display are by famous Belgian artists. The Bourse station features a revolving ceiling sculpture by Pol Bury and a dream-like painting of tram passengers by the great Surrealist Paul Delvaux. At Comte de Flandre, 16 soaring bronze figures by Paul Van Hoeydonck, titled *16 x Icarus*, invade the tunnel. The dazzling adventures of Belgium's comic-strip hero Tintin de Hergé are found covering the walls of the Stockel station.

The city's public transport company, STIB, publishes a brochure describing the art on display in the metro, with several suggested itineraries to follow.

When Belgians do things, they do them with a passion. Where else would you be able to choose from nearly 500 different domestic beers, or eat mussels cooked in 20 different styles? The countless restaurants and bars in the city pay testament to Brussels' love of the good life, and you should many opportunities to join the informal party.

Even King Leopold II caught the collecting 'bug'. He used money from his personal fortune to construct the vast and varied collection of the Royal Museum of Central Africa, personally supervising the design of the building that now houses it.

This passion has also extended to collecting, with a multitude of museums for the visitor to explore. Although many attractions can be found in the compact city centre, many others are located within the 19 *communes* or separate small towns that make up the Brussels-Capital Region. These are only a short tram ride away, or one or two stops on the metro. Each commune has a very particular character – from tree-lined bourgeois districts to gritty working-class neighbourhoods. As Europe has extended a helping hand to refugees from many countries, some areas now have burgeoning African, Asian and Arab populations. Exploring at least one of these *communes* allows you to discover more of the real Brussels; for underneath its charms – the majestic old buildings, impressive museum collections and pretty streets – the city has a complex and alluring personality.

Brussels is full of surprises. City dwellers have vast swathes of forest to enjoy, just a tram ride from the city centre. To those who expect bland Euroland, Brussels presents a historical time capsule. And to those who imagine a living museum, they discover a 21st-century society thoroughly in tune with the 'now'. Allow yourself to enjoy all this about Brussels; it's rare to find a place where this combination works so well.

A BRIEF HISTORY

In 57BC, Julius Caesar came to Belgium and, after a great deal of trouble with a population he described as 'the bravest of all the peoples of Gaul', conquered the country. At that time, Brussels did not yet exist as a city, although two Roman roads had been built through its present site (one of which is still called chaussée Romaine). From the evidence of the bronzes, coins and funeral urns found, a number of dignitaries and officers had villas constructed in the area some decades later. During the 450 years of Roman rule, the Belgae of the southern region became heavily Latinised, while the north was left in the end to Germanic tribes.

Brussels first appeared on the scene around AD 600 when St Géry, the Bishop of Cambrai, is said to have built a church at the small settlement here. At this time and later, it was known variously as Brosella, Brucella, Bruocsella, Bruohsella, Bruesella and Borsella, with as many different meanings suggested by historians. Selections include 'stork's nest' and 'dwelling near the bridge', but the most generally accepted seems to be 'dwelling in the marshes'. This supposedly refers to three swampy islands in the now paved-over River Senne, on which the first castle and church were built.

Local hero: crusader Godfrey of Bouillon, on place Royale

The Middle Ages
The foundation of the city proper dates back officially to AD 979, when a fortress was erected here by Charles,

Duke of Lorraine, the brother of Carolingian King Lothaire of France. In the following century, the town began to take shape when, in 1047, Count Lambert II of Louvain built a new castle on the Coudenberg Heights (today called place Royale), surrounded by a group of houses within a walled compound. The lack of space inside meant that less-fortunate artisans and peasants were left unprotected outside the ramparts, thus laying the foundations for the long struggle between the city's haves and have-nots.

In the 12th century, Brussels rose to prominence in the province of Brabant, gaining in prosperity due to its role as a centre of gold and silversmithing and as a station on the busy commercial route between the thriving trading centres of Cologne and Bruges. By 1235 the city's administration was in the hands of an oligarchy of seven patrician families known as *lignages*. Each contributed an *échevin,* or alderman, to serve

The River Senne

Most major cities have a body of water nearby. They may be seaports, or set on river mouths, or at crossing points on rivers inland. But Brussels does not have a river. Or does it?

Well, in fact, it does. The city was originally founded on the River Senne, whose path cut directly through the centre of the old town. However, when the river became dirty and polluted following the Industrial Revolution, the people of Brussels decided on a novel and innovative solution; they would simply put the river out of sight. Work began in 1867 and was allied with a comprehensive plan by Burgomaster Anspach to create a number of fine boulevards in the newly created landscape above. A series of culverts confined the waters and a network of sewers drained effluent from all parts of the city. Finally, the river disappeared under brick arcades, although it still flows to the present day.

on the council. Brussels expanded its trade in precious metals with international orders for minting coins. It also started a prosperous textile industry using wool imported from England. However, with male workers demanding ever-higher wages and better working conditions, the lords began to look elsewhere for labour, and a number of *béguinages* (communities of religious lay women) were established, partly as a source of cheap and docile workers.

Porte de Hal, the city's only surviving medieval gate

The Brussels bourgeoisie was already growing prosperous and willful. In 1291 Duke Jean I had to make tax and toll concessions to their municipal treasury. In an attempt to forestall the problems of dealing with recalcitrant artisans, the ruling oligarchy claimed the right of approval over the formation of the craft guilds – a restriction that strongly riled the artisans.

The Brussels craftsmen staged a revolt demanding a greater say in city government. Some 36 professional groups were each allowed to send representatives to administer the town's affairs. However, Brussels' first attempt at democracy came to an abrupt end just three years later, when the army of Duke Jean II and the patrician cavalry of the *lignages* defeated the artisans in the bloody battle of Vilvoorde (1306). For the next 50 years the artisans were forbidden to bear arms, and uprisings rumbled on until guild privileges were gradually reinstated for certain professions.

The Burgundians

At the end of the 14th century the dukes of Burgundy took control of Brussels from their seat in Bruges, and under them good times were to be had. However, the demand for Brussels cloth declined, as at the same time textiles manufactured in England became increasingly competitive. By 1430 Brussels cloth had practically disappeared from international markets. With no work, many artisans were forced to leave the city, and the population declined. Brussels compensated for the collapse of the textile industry by turning to tapestry weaving, for which it again became renowned. The best of the Brussels weavers were recruited, and demand for their skills became intense. With demand rising for other skills as well, the craft guilds began to reform and gain strength.

Jan Van Eyck, remembered in Bruges

The Burgundian era was a golden age for the arts. Jan van Eyck, Rogier van der Weyden, Hans Memling and Dirk Bouts were only the best known of a superb group of 15th-century Flemish painters. Civic pride was reflected in the great Gothic town halls that sprang up all across Belgium, though none ever surpassed Brussels' own great jewel in the Grand-Place, surrounded by equally grand guild houses.

The dukes – Philip the Bold and Philip the Good –

asserted their supremacy with pageants and great festivities to keep the people happy. However, their dominance began to disintegrate in wars with Louis XI of France, and before long the city was beset with revolts, famine and plague. Charles the Bold, Philip the Good's successor, was in turn succeeded by his daughter Mary, who married Maximilian of Austria and thus brought the Habsburgs to Brussels.

Charles the Bold

Habsburg Rule

In 1515 Maximilian's grandson, the future Charles V, made his *Joyeuse Entrée* into Brussels as its new archduke. He moved into the palace on the Coudenberg, which was to be his only fixed residence during his peripatetic reign as king of Spain and Holy Roman Emperor. As Bruges lost its influence, Brussels became the capital of the Low Countries (roughly following the borders of what is now Belgium and Holland), as well as a great European centre of trade and culture.

The renowned Dutch philosopher Erasmus also enjoyed the city's pleasant atmosphere, and Pieter Bruegel the Elder came to Brussels to paint his marvellous studies of life in the Low Countries. Brussels' thriving trade in luxury goods at this time was enhanced by the vogue of its lace-makers and the expertise of its highly prized gunsmiths.

The *Ommegang*, or 'walk-around', the most spectacular of Brussels' festivities, gave the resident Renaissance nobility and gentry a chance to show off their riches in a procession around the city. Originally a religious celebration of a miraculous statue of the Virgin (brought to the city in 1348), it soon became an undisguised assertion of the nobility's civic authority. The *Ommegang* is still held every year in early July in the Grand-Place. It was at the event, in 1549, when Charles V proudly introduced his son from Spain to the citizens of Brussels; in 1555, Charles abdicated in his son's favour. The Belgians viewed the new King Philip II with suspicion.

Inquisitions, Shells and Beheadings

During Charles' reign, Calvinists had arrived in Brussels, and the people of the Low Countries embraced the Reformation with enthusiasm. Soon, the spiritual rebellion against Catholicism became identified with the nationalist rebellion against Spanish rule, and discontent grew. Charles only dimly perceived the seriousness of this threat to Spanish power and was lax in enforcing his powers. However, Philip, who disliked his northern subjects, was less easygoing. He brought in the inquisitors and surrounded himself with Spanish soldiers, and blood began to flow.

Nationalist resistance was led by William of Nassau, Prince of Orange. Philip, who in 1559 headed back to Spain, sent the Duke of Alba – known as the 'bloody duke' – to quash the revolt. Two leading landowners, counts Egmont and Hornes, more nationalists than rebels, were executed in the Grand-Place in 1568. However, the Prince of Orange was able to drive out the Spanish in 1576, whereupon Brussels enacted ferocious anti-Catholic legislation. In 1581

> **Count Egmont is remembered not just through the famous statue of him and Hornes on place du Petit-Sablon, but also through a play written by Goethe and an overture, *Egmont*, by Beethoven (opus 84).**

the Catholic religion itself was simply 'abolished.'

This outraged Philip, who sent a large army, under the command of Alexander Farnese, to re-occupy the city. The southern provinces of the Low Countries returned to Spain and Catholicism, but the northern provinces (now the Netherlands) succeeded in breaking away and remained largely Protestant. Brussels saw a flood of Jesuits, monks and nuns to reinforce the Catholic Counter-Reformation.

Under the rule of Philip's daughter, Archduchess Isabella, and her husband, Archduke Albert of Austria, Brussels returned to a general

Statue of counts Egmont and Hornes in place du Petit-Sablon

semblance of order (1599–1633). Life in the capital became quite fashionable, with a constant flow of ambassadors, generals, bishops and cardinals bringing a new cosmopolitan air to the court of the governors-general around the Sablon quarter. The spirit of the age found great artistic expression in the sumptuous contours of Flemish Baroque, which reached its peak with the magnificent paintings of Peter Paul Rubens.

At this time, Brussels was a haven for political exiles – Marie de Medici, Christina of Sweden, the dukes of Bouillon and Vendôme and the sons of Charles I of England. However, by the end of the century it was not quite so safe. In 1695 Louis XIV of France took his revenge for the Dutch and

English shelling of his coastal towns with the wanton bombardment of Brussels. Marshal de Villeroy's army of 70,000 men occupied Anderlecht and set up its cannons at the gate of Ninove. For two days, shells and cannonballs fell on some 4,000 buildings, killing 1,000 people, yet the city did not surrender. The Grand-Place was badly damaged, yet the Town Hall's superb belltower survived.

Revolution to Revolution

In 1701 a dynastic wrangle brought war in Europe, and in the peace that followed, control of the southern Low Countries passed to the Austrian Habsburgs. The subsequent period of growth in Belgium was subsidised by trade links controlled by Vienna. Emperor Joseph II ruled Belgium in the last part of the 18th century with a form of enlightened despotism. His religious reforms and judicial liberalisation upset the profoundly conservative Belgians, and the centralised Vienna-controlled administration jarred with its habit of local autonomy, and nowhere more so than in Brussels.

This was at a time when the Americans had thrown off the British yoke, and the French were getting rid of their royal one. In January 1790 the old patrician families of Brussels staged a revolt, which drove the Austrians out and restored their ancient privileges under the 'Etats Belges Unis' (United Belgian States). The revolutionary regime was short-lived: in December, the Austrians returned, only to be ousted in 1792 by the French Revolutionary army. In 1793 the French decided simply to annex Belgium. Their influence was mixed. Increased trade with France brought more affluence, but museums and libraries were pillaged, and many able-bodied men were press-ganged into the Revolutionary army.

In the winter of 1813–14, Brussels saw the French troops depart, only for them to be replaced by a procession of Russians, Prussians, Dutch and, finally, by the British, waiting for orders to go into battle with Napoleon in 1815. The rendezvous was around 20km (12 miles) away, at Waterloo, on 18 June.

Napoleon's defeat and the resulting Congress of Vienna brought 16 years of Dutch rule to Belgium, resurrecting old tensions and creating new ones. During Napoleon's rule, the national language was French. Even in Flanders, French was the language of the nobility and bourgeoisie. King William of Orange introduced Dutch, previously spoken only by the lower ranks of society, into schools, municipal government and courts. French-speaking teachers were upset by the imposition of Dutch and taught the sciences in Latin. Catholics were upset by the removal of schools from church control, and the liberals were upset by press censorship. Brussels was ready for another revolution.

Colonne du Congrès, commemorating independence

Independence At Last

With Paris overthrowing its monarch in July 1830, revolt was in the air. In August liberal journalists were active in Brussels, and workers were demonstrating against low pay and poor living conditions. At a performance of Daniel Auber's opera *La Muette de Portici* on 25 August, the rousing aria *Amour Sacré de la Patrie* (Sacred Love of the Fatherland) raised the blood of the bourgeois audience. Belgians of all classes came out on to the

streets in a series of civil disturbances. Rioters attacked the Palais de Justice, and sacked the homes of government ministers, while the police and army stood idly by. In September, King William sent troops to Brussels, and there were many casualties on both sides; when Belgium's independence was recognised on 21 July 1831, the keys of the capital were handed over to the country's new king, Leopold of Saxe-Coburg.

With independence came phenomenal economic growth but also social, political and religious conflicts. Tensions were high between Catholics and liberals, and between Flemings (Dutch-speaking Belgians in the north) and Walloons (French-speaking Belgians in the south). Conservative Catholic provinces resisted universal suffrage and so maintained control over the government. This fuelled their fight with the liberals of the capital over education and church power. Although Brussels was nominally bilingual, French was increasingly dominant in business and state administration. The Flemings campaigned with increasing indignation for greater use of their language in the universities and law courts.

Throughout the 19th century and particularly during the reign of Leopold II (1865–1909), industrial expansion and imperial adventures in Africa, particularly in the Congo, brought great prosperity to Brussels. There was a flurry of construction, with magnificent mansions and brash commercial buildings rising up along the wide avenues and boulevards. As ever, the products of the luxury industries – textiles, furniture, lace, fine porcelain, paper and books – were at a premium.

Leopold II

Brussels was once again a safe refuge for political exiles, notably from Poland, Italy, France and Russia. Germany's Friedrich Engels and Karl Marx (who were expelled from Paris in 1845) organised the socialist German Workers' Club at Le Cygne on the Grand-Place (now a high-class restaurant). The two men wrote the *Communist Manifesto* here, and then were kicked out of Belgium in 1848, when it was feared that their writings and ideas might reproduce the latest Paris Revolution. There was also an explosion of artistic achievement in the capital. Painters including James Ensor, Félicien Rops and Fernand Khnopff came together in the Groupe des XX in 1883.

Art Nouveau staircase in the Musée Horta *(see page 51)*

Brussels was also a major centre of Art Nouveau architecture under the leadership of both Victor Horta and Paul Hankar.

World Wars and International Leadership

Belgium's historic vulnerability to invasion was displayed again in August 1914, when Kaiser Wilhelm's German armies occupied Brussels. The capital put up a heroic passive resistance, and when the Germans were defeated, Belgium expressed its new-found sense of national unity in the introduction of universal suffrage, the right to strike, a Flemish university and, finally, a truce in the church-school conflict. In the

1930s there was the emergence in Brussels, as in other European capitals, of new fascist groups drawing on social discontent and primitive chauvinism. The fascist leader Léon Degrelle achieved that which had eluded all other Belgian leaders: he united Catholics, liberals and socialists in a combined effort to defeat him, resoundingly, in the 1937 elections. These grim times offered the best breeding ground for a flight into the Surrealist art of René Magritte and Paul Delvaux, and the inspired comic-strip escapism of Hergé's *Tintin*.

Then came World War II and another German occupation. The Nazi invaders found a few fascist collaborators to prepare Belgium for integration into the Reich, and King Leopold III caused controversy with his passive acceptance of the invasion.

After the war Belgium held a referendum in which King Leopold gained a majority of 58 percent. However, not having a majority in each province, he refused to be reinstated and was succeeded in 1951 by his son Baudouin. While Flemings and Walloons continued to squabble, Belgium took on a new role as the internationalist capital of Western Europe and the Atlantic alliance. In 1957 the EEC (now the European Union) established its headquarters in Brussels. The following year the city staged a very successful World's Fair based on the theme of building a better world for mankind, and in 1960 divested itself of its African colonies.

NATO moved its headquarters to Brussels in 1967, and the city subsequently attracted around a quarter of a million permanent foreign residents to work in military organisations and the multinational offices of commerce. In the 1980s and 1990s, while the Belgian government introduced regional government to allow greater local decision-making, Brussels continued in its role as the central lynchpin in Europe. As the EU expands to the east, the city's role as the focal point for the continent continues to develop.

Historical Landmarks

AD 979 Founding of the city with the building of a fortress.

1047 Construction of the first city wall.

1303 Uprising of craftsmen demanding greater say in city government.

1401 Construction of the Town Hall begins.

1406 Dukes of Burgundy take control of Brussels.

1515 The future Charles V becomes Archduke of Brabant.

1531 Brussels becomes the capital of the Spanish Netherlands.

1555 Charles V abdicates. Brussels is subject to Philip II of Spain.

1568 Belgian counts Egmont and Hornes beheaded for high treason.

1576 Under the Prince of Orange Brussels revolts and drives out the Spanish, but the latter re-occupy the city in 1585.

1599 Archduchess Isabella (daughter of Philip II) and her husband move to Brussels and restore order in the city.

1695 Louis XIV of France bombards Brussels.

1713 Under the Treaty of Utrecht, Brussels becomes subject to Austria.

1789 Brabant Revolution drives out the Austrians, but is crushed the following year by Austria and France.

1794 Belgium is annexed by France.

1815 The French are defeated at Waterloo. Congress of Vienna cedes Belgium to the Netherlands; William of Orange is crowned.

1830 Belgian Revolution begins in Brussels, leading to independence.

1831 Leopold of Saxe-Coburg is made first king of the Belgians.

1914–18 World War I: most of Belgium is occupied by German army.

1940–5 World War II: Belgium is again occupied by Germany.

1951 King Leopold III abdicates in favour of his son, Baudouin.

1957 The EEC (European Union) makes its headquarters in Brussels.

1967 NATO's headquarters are moved to Brussels.

1993 King Baudouin is succeeded by Albert II.

1994 Brussels-Capital becomes one of three federal regions in Belgium.

1995 Brabant province, surrounding Brussels, separates into Dutch-speaking Flemish Brabant and French-speaking Walloon Brabant.

2002 The euro replaces the Belgian franc as the national currency.

WHERE TO GO

The city of Brussels is, in fact, made up of 19 *communes* or boroughs, each with its own town council, administration and police force. Every borough has a distinctive character based on its history, major industry and social make-up. The central borough is the only one called Brussels, but most people travelling to the city know the metropolitan conurbation as a whole by this name.

A well-organised, integrated and cheap public transport system makes greater Brussels easy to explore. Central Brussels is compact and, with comfortable footwear, is a perfect destination for walking.

This guidebook divides the city into a number of easy-to-follow sections, taking central Brussels first and then exploring the highlights of the surrounding *communes*, as well as the battlefield at Waterloo only 15km (9 miles) from the city. We include a number of excursions to explore the towns and cities of Antwerp, Bruges and Ghent.

In the bilingual city of Brussels, street and building names appear in both French and Dutch, and, for simplicity, we have used only the French (spoken by 85 percent of the population). For Flanders, where Dutch prevails, we have followed the local practice in citing place names.

THE HEART OF THE CITY

In the Middle Ages, Brussels was surrounded by a protective wall broken by seven ports or gates. Inside the wall is an area of 3km by 2km (2 miles by 1.5 miles), a network of narrow cobbled streets developed with Coudenberg Palace on the hill marking the city's highest point. When Napoleon Bona-

control of Brussels in 1799, he decided to tear
all and create wide boulevards around the city.
exist today as the *petite ceinture* or inner ring
to six-lane highway. It is the *petite ceinture* that,
most part, creates the boundary between the *commune* of Brussels and the surrounding *communes* of the city.

The Grand-Place

There are some places in the world where no matter how wonderful you hear they are, nothing prepares you for seeing them.
The **Grand-Place** is one such place. The beauty is almost
overwhelming, the skill of the masons awe-inspiring. Yet the
square also has a very human quality, with numerous cafés
where you can sit and watch the world go by.

The Grand-Place has long been the heart of the city. Its
Dutch name, Grote Markt, indicates that it was developed as

The Maison du Roi fronts one side of the Grand-Place

the main marketplace of the city. This part of town became Brussels' commercial heartland at the end of the first millennium, when the marshes of the St-Géry area were drained, creating land for building.

Markets grew up haphazardly, but towards the end of the 13th century, it was clear that a large open area would have to be planned, and houses were demolished to create the space. The foundation stone of the Hôtel de Ville (Town Hall) was laid in 1401 and powerful corporations followed, building their guild houses close to this symbol of secular power.

These buildings were already 200 years old when the League of Augsburg – an alliance between the United Provinces (Holland), Britain, Spain and Germany – went to war with the French under Louis XIV, the Sun King. In 1695, Louis ordered the bombardment of Brussels. On 13 August, 70,000 men laid siege to the walls, and cannonballs began to rain down, devastating the Grand-Place. Only the spire of the Hôtel de Ville and the façades of three houses remained intact.

In the aftermath of this devastation, the town council decided that a new Grand-Place would be planned and controlled. It approved or vetoed the design of each house fronting the square, resulting in the Grand-Place we see today.

The Hôtel de Ville

The **Hôtel de Ville** (Town Hall; guided tours in English: Apr– Sept Tues and Wed 3.15pm, Sun 10.45am and 12.15pm; Oct–Mar Tues and Wed 3.15pm; admission fee), resplendent following major renovation work in the late 1990s, is a magnificent building, whose construction sent an important message about the power that ruled Brussels at the time. While other communities were concentrating their efforts on erecting grand religious buildings, the leaders of Brussels chose to celebrate the civic side of life. The design is an amalgam of covered market and fortified mansion, and each façade was

> **Between March and October, the Grand-Place hosts a flower market (Tues–Sun). It is also the venue of many Brussels festivals, such as the annual Burgundian Ommegang parade in July, when the guilds and corporations gather to celebrate their illustrious histories.**

rebuilt to the original plans following the bombardment of 1695. The 96-m (312-ft) tower, dating from the 1450s, replaced an earlier belfry. A statue of the Archangel Michael, the city's patron, tops the tower. A series of first-floor galleries and arcades brings coherence to these two separate elements. The Lion Staircase, which now forms the main entrance, was added later (the lion statues in 1770). The coving around the portal features sculptures of eight prophets, while the friezes between the first and second floors depict leading ducal luminaries.

The interior is equally attractive. The highly decorated meeting hall is still home to the council of the *commune*, while the Hall of Viershaer, or Court Room, is also used for civil weddings. One wall of the David and Bathsheba Room is filled with a large tapestry dated at 1520, showing Bathsheba at the fountain. Walls in corridors and halls pay tribute in sculpture and paintings to the guildsmen who brought the town prosperity, and the royal families who brought it power. You will find the Tourist Office of Brussels on the ground floor.

Houses of the Dukes and Guilds

Travelling from the Hôtel de Ville in a clockwise direction around the Grand-Place, the first highlight is No. 7, **Le Renard** (meaning 'the fox', in French), or House of the Haberdashers, built in 1699. The name refers to Mr Vos (Dutch for fox), who lived here. It is adorned with statues representing the four continents known at that time, and Justice blindfolded. **Le Cornet**, next door at No. 6, was the boatmen's guild house and has a superb Italianate-Flemish frontage designed by Antoine Pastorana. At No. 5, **La Louve** (1696) is famed for a statue of Romulus and Remus being suckled by a she-wolf (*la louve*), which gives the house its name. Above this are four statues representing Truth, Falsehood, Peace and Discord. **Le Sac** at No. 4, the House of Coopers and Cabinetmakers, has one of the façades that remained standing after the French bombardment. Much of it dates from the 1640s, although Pastorana added the upper ornamentation. The house takes its name from the frieze

Maison du Roi detail

of a man taking something out of a *sac* (bag), which can be found above the door. No. 3, **La Brouette** (The Wheelbarrow) was House of the Tallow or Grease-merchants, and is now a café. On the corner is **Le Roy d'Espagne** (King of Spain's House), which belonged to the guild of bakers. Its classical lines have been attributed to the architect and sculptor Jean Cosyn, and the octagonal dome that tops it – crowned with a gilded weathervane symbolising Fame – adds elegance to the square. Le Roy d'Espagne is now a café.

We now turn to the northern side of the square, opposite the Hôtel de Ville. This is dominated by the large and ornate **Maison du Roi** (King's House), built on the site of the Bread Market between 1515 and 1536. The rights to this piece of

Beer-making at the Musée de la Brasserie (Brewing Museum)

land passed through the dukes of Burgundy to King Charles V, hence the name of the house. In the 1870s, Burgomaster Charles Buls wanted to redesign the house. Architect Pierre-Victor Jamaer retained the Gothic style, adding the flamboyant tower and arcades. Although the overworked façade is not to everyone's taste, you should enjoy the **Musée de la Ville de Bruxelles** (Museum of the City of Brussels; open Tues–Sun 10am–5pm; admission fee) inside. Its rooms have exhibits relating to all aspects of the city's urban development and political and social history. It also displays original statuary from the Hôtel de Ville. The art collection includes works by Pieter Bruegel the Elder and Peter Paul Rubens, but the biggest attraction is the display of some 800 ornate costumes worn by that naughty little Brussels mascot, the Manneken-Pis statue *(see page 35)*, on the top floor.

Three narrow guild houses sit beside the Maison du Roi. No. 28, **La Chambrette de l'Amman** (House of the Amman), was the house of the duke's representative on the Town Council in medieval times. The middle house, **Le Pigeon**, was home to Victor Hugo in 1851. **La Chaloupe d'Or** (Golden Longboat, 1697) is easily recognisable; it is topped by a statue of St Boniface. Originally the House of the Tailors, it is also now a café.

On the eastern side of the square, you will find **La Maison des Ducs de Brabant** (House of the Dukes of Brabant). This façade of harmonious design is in fact six houses and is named for the figures decorating it rather than its former owners.

Three houses lead back toward the Hôtel de Ville. **L'Arbre d'Or** (Golden Tree) at No. 10 is the House of the Brewers – look for gilded emblems of hops and wheat – and has a small museum of brewing, the **Musée de la Brasserie** (open Apr–Nov daily 10am–5pm; Dec–Mar Sat–Sun noon–5pm; admission fee) in the basement. The two rooms juxtapose modern brewing methods with those of days gone by. A refreshing beer is included in the admission price. **Le Cygne** (The Swan), next door at No. 9, is now one of the best restaurants in the city. Originally, it housed the butcher's guild before becoming a tavern and surrogate home to political theorists Karl Marx and Friedrich Engels. It was here in 1848 that they finalised the *Communist Manifesto*, though they had both made a promise not to become involved in politics when they were offered asylum in Belgium. **L'Etoile** (The Star) completes the vista. This house, the smallest on the square, was demolished when rue Charles Buls was

The sign for Le Cygne

Musée du Costume

widened and replaced with a second floor supported by arcades. Below the arcades you'll find a reclining bronze statue of **Everard 't Serclaes**, depicted in the throes of death. He was murdered in 1388 for defending Brussels against powerful ducal enemies. This effigy is considered to bring continued good luck to the people of the city. Rub his arm and the nose of his dog to ensure your share of good fortune.

L'Ilot Sacré

The Grand-Place is surrounded by a medieval warren of narrow streets. Their names tell of the activities that took place here in days gone by: Marché-aux-Fromages (Cheese Market), Marché-aux-Herbes (Herb and Grassmarket) and Marché-aux Poulets (Chicken Market). This really was the commercial heart of the city. At the beginning of the 19th century, the area was cut by wide boulevards, created when the River Senne was culverted and arcaded *(see page 14)*. The name L'Ilot Sacré or Sacred Isle was conjured up to protect it from redevelopment in the 20th century.

One street south of Grand-Place is rue Violette, home to the **Musée du Costume et de la Dentelle** (Costume and Lace Museum; open Mon–Tues and Thur–Fri 10am–12.30pm and 1.30–5pm, Sat–Sun 2–5pm; admission fee). Two 18th-century brick gabled houses provide the backdrop to a fine collection of Belgian fashions and lace from the 19th and 20th centuries. Further south, at the corner of rue de l'Etuve and rue du Chêne, is Brussels' most famous statue, the **Manneken-Pis** *(see below)*.

North of the Grand-Place you can stroll through the **Galeries Royales St-Hubert**. Completed in 1847 this beautiful shopping arcade (in fact three separate, but connected arcades) was one of the first of its kind in Europe; nowadays, it features the best in Brussels' labels. Beautiful glass ceilings allow light to flood the walkways. The Galeries intersect rue des Bouchers, a pedestrian-only street peppered with restaurants and one of the most atmospheric places to eat on a summer evening.

Taking the western route out of the Grand-Place along rue au Beurre (Butter Street), look out for the Dandoy shop on your left. This family-run business, started in 1829, is a Brussels institution. Stop by for delicious marzipan and *speculoos* biscuits before you start your itinerary, and, in summer, try the refreshing ice cream. At the end of rue au

---

Manneken-Pis

Why are large crowds always gathered at the corner of rue de l'Etuve and rue du Chêne? There are almost more cameras here than at a Hollywood premiere. This is the site of Manneken-Pis, the irreverent little statue whose method of delivering water to the fountain below embodies the somewhat offbeat attitude of the average native *Bruxellois*.

The tiny chap is renowned for his wardrobe of around 800 suits – the first one was a gift from the Elector of Bavaria in 1698 – though you may find him naked when you visit. He has been kidnapped three times: once in 1745 by the English, and again in 1747 by the French. On the third and last occasion, in 1817, Manneken-Pis was found broken in pieces. In fact, the statue you see today is a replica of one that was fashioned from the fragments.

> **Bourse metro station plays host to Scientastic, an interactive attraction where you can learn all about the world of science through hands-on experiments, tricks and illusions. It's great for children of all ages.**

Beurre, you will find the rear façade of the ornate **Bourse** (Stock Exchange) directly ahead. A relatively recent Brussels monument, it was completed in 1873 on the site of a former convent.

In a busy part of town, the adjacent 11th-century Romanesque **Eglise St-Nicolas** (Church of St Nicholas) is a quietly spiritual oasis. Refurbished in Gothic style in the 14th century and rebuilt several times since, the handsome little church still shows traces of its original rough construction.

Underneath rue de la Bourse, remains of 13th-century Brussels were discovered some years ago. For several seasons, archaeologists have been working at the site, which has been designated the **Bruxella 1238 Museum** and offers a fascinating view on the early development of the city. The main entrance of the Bourse sits on boulevard Anspach, a wide street created after the River Senne was tamed *(see page 14)* and named after the Burgomaster of the time, Jules Anspach. This separated L'Ilot Sacré from the oldest areas of the city, centred on the marketplace at **place St-Géry**. The fine covered market hall (1881) in the square is now an arts centre, surrounded by trendy bars and restaurants.

Place de la Monnaie to Place de Brouckère

North of the Bourse is **place de la Monnaie**, where the Belgian Revolution started in 1830 – crowds rushed out of the **Théâtre Royal de la Monnaie** after hearing Auber's stirring opera *La Muette de Portici*. **Place des Martyrs**, just a little way north, commemorates those who died in the fight for self-determination in 1830. The buildings are in the Classical style and were constructed in the 1770s, though a number of monuments were added in the 1870s and 1880s. You can reach it by going along rue Neuve, a busy shopping street full of European 'high-street' names.

From place de la Monniae, it is only a short walk to **place de Brouckère**, created in the late 1800s as a homage to the grand squares of Paris. Anspach wanted his new city to rival the French capital and held a competition to make sure the buildings on the square were the finest possible. Today, many have been replaced by more modern structures and those that remain are somewhat lost in a sea of neon. Place de Brouckère is one of the city's entertainment centres, and the terrace café of the Métropole hotel is one of the places to see and be seen.

The Cathedral

The **Cathédral des Sts-Michel-et-Gudule** (open Mon–Fri 8am–6pm, Sat–Sun 8.30am–6pm; cathedral free; admission fee to crypt, treasury and archaeological zone) is located a few minutes' walk to the northeast of the Grand-Place. The cathedral was founded in 1047 and dedicated to the Archangel Michael. Gudule was a saint from Flanders, and her relics were kept in the chapel at St-Géry until being transferred here. The choir dates from the 13th century, and

Sts-Michel-et-Gudule interior

the nave was added in the 14th century. The church was elevated to cathedral status only in 1962.

The approach to the cathedral has been landscaped, and a flight of steps was added in 1860 to make the most of the views of the ornate 15th-century façade. The twin towers are by Jan van Ruysbroeck, who also designed the tower on the Town Hall. Majestic stained-glass windows depict members of the Burgundian and Spanish ruling families, along with fine biblical scenes. Above the choir are five windows depicting Louis II and his wife Marie of Habsburg, while the windows of the northern transept show Charles V and his wife Isabella of Portugal. A number of royals, including Charles of Lorraine, are buried in the chancel. The pulpit is perhaps the most ornate element in the cathedral. The depiction of Adam and Eve being driven from the Garden of Eden was carved in 1699 by Hendrik Verbruggen of Antwerp. Below ground are

Art Nouveau setting for the Centre Belge de la Bande-Dessinée

the remains of two round towers (*c*.1200), corners of the original church dating from the 10th century, which were discovered during renovation work in the 1980s.

> The actual name of Tintin's creator was Georges Rémi. Hergé is the French pronunciation of his initials rendered in reverse.

Comic Strip Centre

On the northern outskirts of L'Ilot Sacré, on rue des Sables, is a museum commemorating Belgium's immense contribution to the development of the comic strip as an art form. The **Centre Belge de la Bande-Dessinée** (Belgian Comic Strip Centre; Tues–Sun 10am–6pm; admission fee) acts as a resource centre for studies into the genre and has exhibits that bring these comic book and celluloid heroes to life, with *Tintin* and his inventor Hergé taking pride of place. The museum is housed in the Art Nouveau former Waucquez department store, designed and built by Victor Horta in 1906, and faithfully restored.

THE LOWER CITY

West of the Bourse, the Lower City has seen many changes over the last 1,000 years. In the 13th century, a large community of *béguines* (religious lay women) was established in the Convent of Notre-Dame de la Vigne. The women found safety in the order, living in a large walled compound. The compound was ransacked and abolished during the French Revolution, and now only the **Église St-Jean-Baptiste-au-Béguinage** remains.

Following the completion of the Willebroeck Canal between Brussels and Antwerp in 1561, goods could be transported to the city by water. Quays built in what is now the Marché-aux-Poissons (Fish Market) have since been filled in, but the street names still relate to their original purposes: quai aux Briques (bricks) and quai au Bois-à-Brûler (firewood), for

Church of St-Jacques

example. The area has been beautified with fountains and pools. The most central quay reaches as far as place Ste-Catherine with **Église Ste-Catherine** at its centre. This church originates from the 14th century but was rebuilt in 1854. The square is also the location of the Tour Noire (Black Tower), one of the few remains of the original city wall, which was over-restored in the 1800s.

PLACE ROYALE

While the commercial town developed on marshy ground, the families with power lived on Coudenberg (Cold Hill). Today, this part of town still has palaces, but is also home to some of the major museums. To reach the museums, take a route through the **Mont des Arts**, past the statues of King Albert I and his wife Queen Elisabeth facing each other across place de l'Albertine. The Monts des Arts complex was a contentious redevelopment. It was a project to create a centre of arts and learning backed by Leopold II, but resulted in the destruction of a large residential area in the 1890s. Unfortunately, before the rebuilding began, Leopold died, and the project foundered. A large garden area was a temporary solution that lasted until after World War II. The building of the four-million volume **Royal Library** in 1954 and the public records office (begun in 1960) have encased the remaining gardens in stone and concrete.

Once through the gardens, there is a view up to **place Royale**, decorated with a statue of Godefroid de Bouillon, a crusader and ruler of Jerusalem. Behind this you will see the campanile of the **church of St-Jacques-sur-Coudenberg**. This part of the capital was changed greatly by Charles of Lorraine when he became governor of the Low Countries in the mid-1700s. He looked toward Vienna for inspiration and brought together the then-disparate architectural styles of Coudenberg to create a unified suburb. The **apartments of Charles of Lorraine** can be seen in place du Musée in the beautiful Louis XVI Palais de Charles de Lorraine (open Tues–Fri 1–5pm, Sat and 1st Sun of month 10am–5pm; closed last week Aug and last week Dec; admission fee), though Charles died before it was completed. The apartments bear witness to the Habsburg love of luxury and Charles' eye for decor.

As you walk towards place Royale you'll see a splendid Art Nouveau building on your left. This is the **Old England Department Store**, designed in 1899 by Paul Saintenoy. The building has been fully renovated to house the **Musée des Instruments de Musique** (Musical Instruments Museum; open Tues, Wed and Fri 9.30am–5pm, Thur 9.30am–8pm, Sat–Sun 10am–5pm; admission fee). It houses a reception area, gift shop and, on the top floor, a café with panoramic views over the city. The museum is a treasure trove of musical instruments, displaying more than 1,500 in 90 groups relating to type and age. On entering, you receive headphones that allow you to listen to a selection of music at each site.

Antique keyboard

Art Museums

From Place Royale, it is easy to see Charles' vision for the area. Turning right down rue de la Régence, on your immediate right are the **Musées Royaux des Beaux-Arts de Belgique** (Royal Museums of Fine Arts; open Tues–Sun 10am–5pm; admission fee), including both historical and modern art. This is one of the finest collections in Europe, started at the behest of Napoleon Bonaparte. It moved into its present location in the court rooms of Charles' palace in 1887. The museum has been updated and thoughtfully designed, with some large open halls for relaxed viewing. Even so, the huge collection takes a long time to see, so take advantage of the on-site café for refreshment if you become tired.

The **Musée d'Art Ancien** (Museum of Historical Art) offers more than 1,200 canvasses, with a wealth of Flemish masters on show. Works by Dirk Bouts (1420–75) and Hans Memling (1439–94) showcase the 1400s, with Memling's *La Vierge et l'Enfant* being particularly notable. Hieronymus Bosch and Gerard David lead into the 1500s. Pieter Bruegel (1527–69), whose realism had a profound influence on art within the Low Countries, is also represented, along with Peter Paul Rubens (1577–1640) and his pupil Antony van Dyck (1599–1641). Works by Frans Hals and Rembrandt are featured, too. In addition, the museum devotes space to the artistic movements that developed at the end of the 19th century, such as Impressionism – the collection includes paintings by Renoir, Monet and Sisley.

The **Musée d'Art Moderne** (Modern Art Museum), a sister gallery to that of the historical collection, concentrates on pieces from the late 19th and 20th centuries. Though you enter through a neo-Classical building, part of the museum is, in fact, built below ground level with a huge central glass wall allowing light into the galleries. Cubist, Fauvist, Abstract and Surrealist artists are represented. The pieces are arranged chronologically and feature Belgian artists such as René Magritte (1898–1967), Rik Wouters and Paul Delvaux (1897–1994), along with work by Picasso, Dalí, Miró, Gauguin and Seurat.

Parc de Bruxelles and Palais Royal

On the south side of the museum is a small sculpture garden; however, if you head north from the museum entrance back across the square, you will see the trees of the **Parc de Bruxelles** ahead. Originally owned by the dukes of Brabant, it has been open land for several centuries. The formal park with ornamental fountains and statuary in the French style was completed in 1835.

On its south side, the garden looks on to the impressive front façade of the **Palais Royal** (Royal Palace), once part of the site of the Palace of the Dukes of Brabant. Construction

When the flag flies over the Palais Royal, the king is in residence

began in 1820 following a disastrous fire, which destroyed the previous building. It was greatly modified under Leopold II during his reign (1865–1909), with several of the chambers and the façade given Classical and Louis XVI-style embellishments. The palace is now used for ceremonial occasions, as the royal family lives at Laeken on the outskirts of the city. If the king is in residence, you will see the Belgian flag fluttering on the flagpole above the entrance.

The palace is open for tours from the end of July to the beginning of September, but if you want to know more about the Belgian royal family, visit the **Musée de la Dynastie** (Dynasty Museum; open Apr–Sept Tues–Sun 10am–6pm; Oct–Mar Tues–Sun 10am–5pm; admission fee), which is housed in the Bellevue Apartments in the east wing of the palace. The rooms still retain their original splendour. Tasteful exhibits have been added to tell the story of each royal reign in chronological order, including both the personal and professional lives of the monarchs. Artefacts include personal belongings and photographs of the royal family. There is also a memorial to the late King Baudouin, who died in 1993.

On the opposite side of the Parc de Bruxelles is the **Palais de la Nation**, which was constructed in 1783. It has been the seat of the Belgian government since 1830.

The **Colonne du Congrès** (Congress Column), on rue Royale, marks Belgium's Independence Revolution in 1830. Atop its 47-m (153-ft) shaft stands a statue of King Leopold I (1790–1865). At its base is the Tomb of the Unknown Soldier.

Travel back towards the old part of the city via rue Baron Horta and you will find the **Palais des Beaux-Arts (Bozar)** on the corner to your left, on rue Ravenstein. Completed in 1928 to a design by Victor Horta, it is much admired for its interior detail. Major cultural events such as the Queen

Elisabeth Music Contests are held here; the foyer holds temporary exhibitions, so something is always happening. Also on rue Baron Horta is the **Musée du Cinéma** (tel: 02-507 8370), which has daily screenings.

LE SABLON

Once a marshy wasteland, this part of Brussels saw large mansions built for the ruling families in the 16th century, but became especially fashionable in the 19th century. Many fine town

Guild statue on place du Petit-Sablon

houses date from this time. Today, it has numerous antiques shops, art galleries, good restaurants and busy bars, which makes it a popular place to browse and have lunch.

From the Beaux-Arts area it is easy to find the Sablon. A short walk south along rue de la Régence brings you to the chapel of **Notre-Dame du Sablon** at the top of **place du Grand-Sablon**. The chapel was built in 1304 by the guild of crossbowmen, and the statue of Our Lady found here is said to have healing properties. The chapel has undergone several extensions and embellishments, the last in the 19th century. You'll discover a marvellous 17th-century Baroque pulpit carved by Marcos de Vos. Since the 15th century, the square in the shadow of the chapel has hosted markets. It is still home to an antiques fair every weekend.

Behind the church and across rue de la Régence is **place du Petit-Sablon**, with its own park, laid out in 1890. It is decorated with wonderful statuary. Each post of the wrought iron fence around the park is topped with the bronze figure of a man portraying a trade guild. Pride of place within the square is taken by a large sculptured tribute to counts Hornes and Egmont, who were beheaded in the Grand-Place in 1568 following unsuccessful protests against the excesses of Spanish rule. Above the square you'll see the **Palais d'Egmont** (1534), once the family home of the Dukes of Egmont, but now housing part of the Belgian Ministry of Foreign Affairs. You can't tour the palace, but you can enjoy the gardens.

LES MAROLLES

Les Marolles is a working-class district that grew on trade and labour skills – coopering and blacksmithing, primarily. The Marolles has never been gentrified (though in recent years this has begun around its edges) and retains a unique atmosphere, its streets filled with hustle and bustle.

Overlooking the whole area is the **Palais de Justice**, a huge edifice that became a *cause célèbre* when its plans were revealed. It was one of the largest buildings in Europe when it was completed in 1883, and a huge sector of the Marolles had to be demolished to make way for it – much to the chagrin of the local people. Everything about the building is on a grand scale, including an entrance porch 42m (150ft) in height.

The rest of the Marolles spreads out to the west and is cut by two main streets. **Rue Haute** is the longest street in Brussels, and one of the oldest. Pieter Bruegel is said to have been born c.1525 in a house at No. 132 that can be dated from that time. Bruegel and other members of his family are buried in **Notre-Dame de la Chapelle** at the city end of rue Haute. Consecrated in 1210, the church underwent renovations in 1421 following a fire, and the Baroque belltower was added after the bombardment of 1695 destroyed an earlier tower. The interior has several fine works, the best being

Flea market at place du Jeu-de-Balle

the memorial to Bruegel (the Elder) by his son Jan. At the *petite ceinture* end of rue Haute, you will find the **Porte de Hal**, the last remaining medieval city gate, saved from destruction because it served as a prison. Built in the 14th century, it was radically altered in the 19th century in the faux-medieval fashion of the day – most of the top embellishments date from this time. The lower original walls have a much simpler design.

The second major street of the Marolles is rue Blaes, which is famed for its flea market (daily except Sunday) at **place du Jeu-de-Balle**. You can buy almost anything here, from furniture and clothes to old 78 records and family photographs. The streets surrounding place du Jeu-de-Balle are dotted with numerous cafés and bars, as well as lots of secondhand stores. Look out for De Skieven Architek, a bar on the square whose name sums up what the people thought of the designer of the Palais de Justice.

BEYOND THE OLD CITY

There are numerous attractions to visit outside the old town and within the other *communes* of the city. Some can be reached on foot, the rest by public transport.

To the East

The area directly east of the old town has perhaps seen the most change in the last 50 years. This area is the heart of the European Union administration, with numerous office buildings housing EU departments, support staff and the diplomatic missions and pressure groups aiming to influence the EU's decisions. As much as 1.2 sq km (0.46 sq miles) of space is taken by the various arms of this one institution.

The headquarters of the European Parliament, **Hémicycle Européen**, is at l'Espace Léopold. (It is often derisively called the *Caprice des Dieux* by Belgians, because of the building's resemblance to the box in which the cheese of the same name is packed.) Its curved glass roof rising to 70m (228ft) can be seen from all around this district, and there are particularly pretty views from **Parc Léopold** at its eastern side.

South of the park you will find the **Institut des Sciences Naturelles** (Natural Sciences Institute). Its museum (open Tues–Fri 9.30am–4.45pm, Sat–Sun and school holidays, except July–Aug, 10am–6pm; admission fee) aims to enhance understanding of the natural world, and is best known for its collection of dinosaurs, particularly a group of more than 30 iguanadons found in southern Belgium in 1905. Several have been reconstructed in upright positions, while others are displayed as they were found lying in the ground.

Just a little way further east from the European headquarters is the **Parc du Cinquantenaire**. When Belgium reached its Golden Jubilee, King Leopold II wanted to celebrate by creating a monument to national pride. He enlisted

Triumphal arch at Parc du Cinquantenaire

the help of architect Gédéon Bordiau who planned a grand
esplanade, formal gardens and a ceremonial arch, with two
wings to house museum and gallery space. However, the
project hit snags and was not complete for the celebrations.
The monumental arch, which features a large bronze entitled
Brabant Raising the National Flag, was completed in 1888,
but the complex was since hit by fire, and one of the wings
has been completely rebuilt in a slightly different style.
Today the Cinquantenaire complex houses three museums. It
is easily reached by metro to Mérode station.

The south wing is home to the **Musée du Cinquantenaire**
(open Tues–Fri 9.30am–5pm; Sat–Sun 10am–5pm; admission
fee), a collection of art and historical artefacts that covers
every civilisation from pre-historic times to the present. The
Roman and Greek remains are particularly fine, with beautiful
mosaics and statuary. Rooms dedicated to earlier near Eastern
civilisation, and ancient Asian and American societies are also

Musée du Cinquantenaire

impressive. Religious relics, furniture, pottery and jewellery are all of exceptionally high quality and thoughtfully displayed. There are over 140 rooms to explore here, so the map given to you at reception is absolutely vital.

In the south hall next door is **Autoworld** (open Apr–Sept daily 10am–6pm; Oct–Mar Mon–Fri 10am–5pm, Sat–Sun 10am–6pm), a collection of more than 450 vehicles. Many early Belgian manufacturers are represented, with a number of pre-1920 Minerva cars and a 1948 Imperia, the last Belgian car produced before vehicle production was swallowed by larger European manufacturers. Almost every maker is represented, including Rolls-Royce, Studebaker and Mercedes. Also on display is the Cadillac used by President Kennedy when he visited Berlin in 1963.

The **Musée Royal de l'Armée et d'Histoire Militaire** (Army and Military History Museum; open Tues–Sun 9am–noon and 1–4.30pm; free) is in the north wing and hall. One of the largest museums of its kind in the world, it covers 10 centuries of military history. In the 19th-century section are uniforms, arms and the personal effects of soldiers from Belgian units, including those of Leopold I. The walls are filled with images of uniformed gentlemen, and shot-torn battle flags hang from the ceiling. Another section features 14th- and 15th-century artefacts, with suits of armour, swords and shields. There are displays of tanks and other vehicles, and an aircraft section including a Spitfire and Hurricane from World War II.

To the South

Avenue Louise, leading southeast from the *petite ceinture*, is a fine thoroughfare, with cafés and restaurants among the department stores and *haute couture* boutiques. There are several Art Nouveau homes on the adjacent residential streets, including the **Musée Horta** (Horta Museum; open Tues–Sun 2–5.30pm; admission fee) on rue Américaine. The building was designed by Victor Horta as a home and studio. It is considered to be the epitome of Art Nouveau architecture in Brussels.

Travelling to the end of avenue Louise (by tram from the Palais de Justice) leads you to the **Bois de la Cambre,** a beautiful park area with lakes and pleasant paths for walking. Just before the park, the former Cistercian **Abbaye de la Cambre** (La Cambre Abbey) is a tranquil retreat, surrounded

---

Art Nouveau

For all the demolition of architectural gems in recent decades, the tide seems to be turning towards preserving what remains of a remarkable heritage. And despite being the capital of so many other things, Brussels is perhaps proudest of being the 'capital of Art Nouveau', having been bequeathed some of the finest architecture of this exuberant turn-of-the-20th-century style. Property 'developers' and local government connivance have conspired to destroy some buildings, but others remain to dazzle the eye.

The foremost proponent of Art Nouveau, a style typified by naturalistic forms and motifs, was Brussels architect Victor Horta, some of whose students continued the tradition. Notable examples of the genre are the Solvay Mansion, the cafés De Ultieme Hallucinatie and Le Falstaff, Magasins Waucquez department store (which houses the Belgian Comic Strip Centre), the Old England department store (which houses the Museum of Musical Instruments), the Tassel House, the florist De Baecker, and townhouses in square Ambiorix and square Marie-Louise.

by an ornamental garden containing fountains and pools and the 13th-century church of **Notre-Dame de la Cambre**. The abbey buildings now house an art school and the National Geographical Institute. The *bois* itself is, in fact, the manicured tip of a much larger natural green area, the **Forêt de Soignes**, Europe's largest beech forest, which was once a royal hunting ground. Here, you'll find acres of trees cut by paths, running tracks, bridle and cycle ways

To the West

West of Brussels is the *commune* of **Anderlecht**. One of the most illustrious men of the Renaissance, Desiderius Erasmus (1469–1536), lived here in a house dating in part from 1468. **Maison d'Erasme** (House of Erasmus; open Tues–Sun 10am–5pm; admission fee) is a fine example of 15th-century architecture and features the writing desk of the philosopher, a Catholic contemporary of Martin Luther, who railed against the strictures of Catholic dogma. The upper floor has a collection of rare books and manuscripts relating to the humanist movement and growing religious strife. The Renaissance room is home to several fine paintings by Hieronymus Bosch and Dirk Bouts. Across the street is the **Anderlecht**

House of Erasmus

Béguinage (open Tues–Sun 10am–noon and 2–5pm; admission fee), founded in 1252. Two cottages can now be visited. They house a small folklore museum.

To the North

Just beyond the *petite ceinture* in the north is the redeveloped Gare du Nord zone,

Situated close to the Anderlecht Béguinage, in a family-owned brewery in rue Gheude, the Musée de la Gueuze (open Mon–Fri 10am–6pm, Sat in spring and autumn; admission fee) celebrates traditional Brussels beers. Perfect on a hot summer's day.

which has attracted a number of hotels and bars and a lot of nightlife to the area. **Place Rogier**, home to theatres, clubs and shopping malls, is the centre of the activity.

Going west from here leads you to the massive **Basilique Nationale du Sacré-Coeur** (National Basilica of the Sacred Heart), in Koekelberg. Begun in 1905 and completed in 1970, this church looks something like a modern take on a Byzantine basilica. A gallery in the prominent dome affords a panoramic view of Brussels.

A couple of minutes walk east from place Rogier is **Le Botanique**, a former botanical garden and glass house dating from 1826, which was transformed into a cultural centre in the 1980s. The interior is spectacular, with the glass houses – complete with plants – forming a link between the various exhibition halls (these host theatre and musical events along with temporary exhibitions).

In 1935 and 1958, Brussels hosted major international exhibitions. The events were held in the north of the city at **Heysel**, where vast exhibition halls were built. Since that time, a number of attractions have developed here. All these can be accessed from the Heysel metro station.

The **Palais des Expositions** is a fine building erected for the 1935 exhibition. However, it is a structure from the 1958

World Fair that captured the hearts of the people and became one of the most popular symbols of Brussels. The recently refurbished **Atomium** (open Apr–Aug daily 9am–8pm; Sept–Mar 10am–6pm; admission fee) was built in the shape of the atomic structure of an iron crystal on a scale of 1:165 billion. Constructed of metal spheres linked by tubes, it was created to symbolise the great advances made in the sciences throughout the 20th century. There is a good view of Brussels and the surrounding countryside from the top sphere, a lofty 102m (332ft) high.

The Atomium is adjacent to **Bruparck**, a large recreational area filled with a variety of activities. Try **l'Océade** for water-based relaxation, or **Kinepolis** with its 26 cinemas showing the latest releases. **Mini-Europe** (open late-Mar–June and Sept daily 9.30am–5pm; July–Aug daily 9.30am–7pm (mid-July–mid-Aug Fri–Sun 9.30am–11pm); Oct–Dec and 1st week Jan 10am–5pm; admission fee) celebrates European union in a light-hearted way. More than 300 of Europe's best-known landmarks have been recreated here in miniature (1:25 scale) to allow you a whistle-stop tour no matter how short your stay. The Grand-Place model alone took 19,000 hours to create. You can visit a 4-m (13-ft) high Big Ben and a 13-m (42-ft) high Eiffel Tower – and press a button that causes the miniature Mount Vesuvius to erupt.

The Royal Estate at Laeken

South of Heysel is the **Domaine Royal de Laeken**, a vast estate and palace, where the royal family has residences. Although the palace is not open to the public, the magnificent **Serres Royales** (Royal Glass Houses) can be visited in April or May. These were built at the behest of Leopold II following his visit to the Crystal Palace in London and other new glass houses of Europe. A monument to this influential monarch has been erected in the parc de Laeken opposite the palace.

Leopold was full of enthusiasm for architectural styles and building methods – a passion that resulted in the construction of two Asian-inspired structures to the north of the palace. The **Pavillon Chinois** (Chinese Pavilion; open Tues–Fri 9.30am–5pm, Sat–Sun 10am–5pm; admission fee), with a carved wooden façade imported from Shanghai, was completed after Leopold's death in 1910. The pavilion now houses a collection of Chinese ceramics. The **Tour Japonaise** (Japanese Tower; open Tues–Fri 9.30am–5pm, Sat–Sun 10am–5pm; admission fee), reached by tunnel from the Chinese Pavilion, was designed and built by Parisian architect Alexandre Marcel. It is now used for exhibitions relating to Japanese art.

In nearby Jette, an unassuming house on rue Esseghem was the home of René Magritte from 1930–54. The **René Magritte Museum** (open Wed–Sun 10am–6pm; admission fee) promotes the painter's work and acts as a research centre.

The Chinese Pavilion at Laeken with a façade from Shanghai

ENVIRONS OF BRUSSELS

Tervuren

You can reach the suburban Flemish village of **Tervuren** by taking tram 44 from Montgomery metro station. The route takes you through the commune of **Woluwe-St-Lambert**, a pretty residential suburb with beautiful parks. It also plays host to the **Musée du Transport Urbain de Bruxelles** (Brussels Urban Transport Museum; open Apr–early Oct Sat–Sun and hols 1.30–7pm; admission fee), directly on the public transport route, for those who enjoy old trams and trolley buses.

Belgian writer Roger Martin du Gard nicknamed Tervuren 'the Versailles of Belgium', and the royal estate here is based on Classical French architectural style and garden design.

In 1897, Leopold II organised a colonial exhibition relating to his expanding lands in the Congo. This proved so success-

Verdant gardens surround the Musée Royal de l'Afrique Centrale

ful that a permanent home was built for the exhi anthropological research centre was instituted. Leopo sonally contracted Frenchman Charles Girault, designer of Petit Palais in Paris, to build the museum. The **Musée Roya de l'Afrique Centrale/Koninklijk Museum voor Midden Afrika** (Royal Museum of Central Africa; open Tues–Fri 10am–5pm, Sat–Sun 10am–6pm; admission fee) on Leuvens-esteenweg is a stunning building surrounded by acres of formal gardens. The exhibits include rather outdated displays of stuffed animals and a collection of species of insects that children seem to find fascinating. The museum also holds a marvellous collection of tribal artefacts from central Africa, including weapons, musical instruments and ceremonial masks. The history of the exploration of Africa is covered, including the issue of slavery. Personal effects of David Livingstone and Henry Morton Stanley are included in this section.

The attractive formal gardens surrounding the museum give way to natural forest and parkland. There is a boating lake with lots of bird life, making Tervuren a relaxing spot to spend a sunny afternoon.

Waterloo

Of the many battles that have taken place on Belgian soil over the centuries, the Battle of **Waterloo** was one of the most important. Its impact on European history was long lasting and it proved to be the final rally for Napoleon in his unsuccessful bid to retake France's leadership. It was during June 1815 that a combined force from Britain, the Low Countries and Prussia began the campaign that would finally destroy the French Emperor. They met in the countryside outside the village of Waterloo on 18 June. By the day's close the French had been routed, and nearly 50,000 men lay dead or wounded on the battlefield.

Travelling to the site today, one can still see how beautiful the countryside must have been. It has changed with the

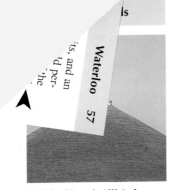

The Lion Mound at Waterloo

addition of a modern four-lane highway (the Brussels outer ring road). However, many of the historic buildings have been preserved as museums devoted to the battle. **La Butte de Lion** (Lion Mound), built on the site in 1826 by the government of the Netherlands, marks the spot where their leader, the Prince of Orange, was wounded. The 40-m (132-ft) mound is topped by a cast iron statue of a lion 4.5m (14ft) in height. Climb the mound to enjoy a panoramic view of the battlefield.

At the base of the mound is a **Visitors' Centre** (Butte de Lion, Visitors' Centre and Panorama open Apr–Sept daily 9.30am–6.30pm; Oct–Mar daily 10am–5pm; separate or combined admission fee; visitors' centre free), which presents an audio-visual exhibit of the battle, including the tactics and movements of the opposing forces and a time frame. Nearby, you will also see the **Panorama de la Bataille** (Panorama of the Battle), a 110m-by-12m (358ft-by-39ft), a painting executed by Louis Dumoulin in 1913 and depicting scenes of one of the most important events of the battle. Across the narrow road is the **Musée des Cires** (Waxworks Museum; open Apr–Nov daily 10am–5pm; Dec–Mar Sat–Sun only; admission fee) containing waxworks of the leading military figures involved in the combat.

Strolling around the battlefield, you'll pass the fortified farms of Hougoumont and La Haie-Sainte, which played crucial roles in the battle. At the southern end of the battlefield is the **Musée Provincial du Caillou** (open Apr–Oct daily 10am–6.30pm; Nov–Mar daily 1–5pm; admission fee), housed in what was Le Ferme Caillou (Caillou Farm), where Napoleon had his headquarters on the eve of the battle. There are a few pieces of memorabilia from the combat, including the skeleton of a hussar found at the site.

The British Duke of Wellington had his headquarters at the inn in the village of Waterloo 3km (1.8 miles) to the north. Restored in 1975, it is now home to the **Musée Wellington** (Wellington Museum; open Apr–Sept 9.30am–6pm; Oct–Mar 10.30am–5pm; admission fee), which also has a section depicting the history of Waterloo itself. There is a room devoted to the Duke of Wellington, containing numerous personal effects. Other rooms are given over to the Dutch and Prussian armies and their heroes, and charts of the battlefield.

Battle of Waterloo

One of many surprising aspects of the Battle of Waterloo is that it did not take place at Waterloo at all, but in rolling fields 4km (2.5 miles) further south, where the road from Brussels, after passing through the Forêt de Soignes and Waterloo, arrives at a low ridge beyond the farm of Mt-Saint-Jean. A traveller taking this route on 18 June 1815 would have run into the French Emperor Napoleon Bonaparte and his 75,000 troops here, doing their headlong best to go in the opposite direction.

More surprising by far is that Napoleon, who won an empire through his supreme grasp of the military art, lost it in the end by putting his head down and charging repeatedly uphill in vain, bloody attempts to shift the Duke of Wellington's 72,000-man army blocking the road to Brussels. 'If my orders are properly executed,' Napoleon told his generals before kicking off the carnage, 'we will sleep tonight in Brussels.' The superb courage of the French soldiers came near to confirming their emperor's prediction. Wellington called the contest 'the nearest run thing you ever saw in your life'.

EXCURSIONS

Antwerp

Where Brussels has developed into Belgium's most important administrative and legislative city, Antwerp (Antwerpen/Anvers), only 40km (30 miles) to the north, has always been its industrial and commercial heart. Founded on the River Scheldt, it was an important staging post on the route from England into central Europe and developed into a large port as early as the Middle Ages. During the Renaissance, Antwerp was one of the cultural capitals of Europe, with the artist Peter Paul Rubens greatly influencing his native town, and philosopher/businessman Christophe Plantin acting as a magnet for advocates of the new sciences.

Walking along the streets of Antwerp today, you quickly become aware of a different atmosphere than that in Brussels. There is a raw energy here, an activity of movement of cargo and goods rather than of paper or files. The city is still one of the largest ports in Europe and the world's centre of diamond polishing.

One cannot fail to find the **Onze-Lieve-Vrouwekathedraal** (Cathedral of Our Lady; open Mon–Fri 10am–5pm, Sat 10am–3pm, Sun 1–4pm, day before a religious holiday 10am–3pm; admission fee), whose great steeple, at 120-m (400-ft), towers above every other building in the compact old town. Built during the 14th and 15th centuries, it is a remarkable Gothic creation,

> **Antwerp is the world's centre for trade in diamonds. Most of the cutting, polishing and trading takes place in the Diamond Quarter, where the offices of the Hoge Raad voor Diamant (Diamond High Council) and the Beurs voor Diamanthandel (Diamond Exchange) stand amid a glittering array of jewellery shops.**

the largest in Belgium, and its interior proportions almost take the breath away. Three Rubens masterpieces decorate the south transept, the north transept and an ambulatory chapel: *Raising of the Cross*, *Descent from the Cross* and *Resurrection* are colourful and dramatic canvasses that give full reign to the artist's prodigious talent. The largest of the cathedral's chapels, St Anthony's, has a beautiful stained-glass window, which dates from 1503; it depicts King Henry VII of England kneeling with his queen and was created to commemorate a commercial deal made

Cathedral of Our Lady, Antwerp

at that time between England and the Low Countries.

A stroll around the outside of the cathedral also reveals a few surprises. The area acted as a commercial centre as well as a religious site and huddling around the base of the structure are buildings as old as the church. These are now tea shops, bars and souvenir shops. Across from the cathedral, with an entrance at Oude Koornmarkt 16, Vlaeykensgang is a tranquil medieval courtyard. In front of the cathedral is the small **Handschoenmarkt** with its cafés. Look out for an ornate well, the **Putkevie**, topped by a statue of Brabo, the hero of Antwerp.

Walking west towards the river will bring you to the **Grote Markt** and the Stadhuis (Town Hall). This square, like the

Antwerp's Grote Markt, with Brabo at its centre

Grand-Place in Brussels, epitomises the power of trade and commerce throughout the history of the city. The mansions that line the Grote Markt were built for the trades' guilds or corporations, which wielded great power during Antwerp's heyday. The most ornate is No. 7, **De Oude Voetboog** (House of the Old Crossbow). At the centre of the Grote Markt is a 19th-century fountain, with a classical depiction of Brabo wielding the severed hand of the giant Antigoon *(see box, right)*.

Antwerp's Town Hall

The **Stadhuis** (Town Hall; guided tours Mon–Wed and Fri–Sat 11am, 2 and 3pm; admission fee) was built in the late 1560s under Cornelius de Vriedt. It has a somber balance in its design, with lines of faux columns atop a ground floor of arched doorways. The central section is pure Flemish in its architectural adornment and was added in the 19th century. Coats of arms of local duchies grace the façade, and a central alcove displays a statute of Our Lady, the protector of the city. Inside, the corridors have colourful dioramas depicting historical council meetings and activities in the chambers. A profusion of marble and well-polished wood gives a feeling of strength and stability. To the south is **Groenplaats**, lined with shops and cafés and sporting a fine statue of Rubens.

After exploring Grote Markt, head towards the river via the beautiful **Vleeshuis** (Butchers' Hall). Built in the 16th century, it looks like a church with a fine façade and spires, but was a guild house and trading hall. When you reach the river, you can take a boat trip downstream to the busy modern harbour to watch cargoes being loaded and unloaded.

Boat trips leave regularly in summer from the dockside at the **Steen**. This 16th-century castle is the oldest remaining structure in Antwerp, and legend has it that it was the home of Antigoon the giant. It later became a prison. Today, it houses the **Nationaal Scheepvaartmuseum** (National Maritime Museum; open Tues–Sun 10am–5pm; admission fee), which has a large collection of maps and charts, navigation equipment and other sea-faring artefacts. Antwerp owes a great deal of its prosperity to the development of sea trade, and the museum is a fitting tribute to the merchant fleet.

Brabo – Antwerp's Hero

Legend tells of how the citizens of Antwerp were being terrorised by an evil giant, Antigoon, who extracted tolls from those who wanted to cross the river. If travellers could not pay, Antigoon would cut off their hands in punishment. Young Silvius Brabo, a relative of Julius Caesar, was brave enough to stand up to the monster and beat him, cutting off his hand as a sign of victory and throwing it into the River Scheldt. His heroics not only saved the whole town from tyranny, but may also have given the town its name – *hand werpen* (hand-throw).

Printing and Art

Walk south of Grote Markt towards the **Plantin-Moretus Museum** (open Tues–Sun 10am–5pm; admission fee) in Vrijdagmarkt. Christopher Plantin was one of the most important craftsmen-businessmen of the late Spanish Empire. His house and neighbouring printing press offer a fascinating insight into the man and the philosophy of this time of great expansion and learning, concentrating on writing and printing. Seven

Rubens' *Education of the Virgin* in the Royal Fine Arts Museum

antique printing presses are still in working order, and there is a collection of rare manuscripts. Pride of place must go to the Biblia Regia (Polyglot Bible), printed between 1568 and 1572 in eight volumes – an epic feat at the time – in Hebrew, Syriac, Aramaic, Latin and Greek. Plantin's family sat for portraits that are displayed on the walls, many of which were painted by Rubens.

More art can be found at the **Koninklijk Museum voor Schone Kunsten Antwerpen** (Royal Fine Arts Museum Antwerp; open Tues–Sat 10am–5pm, Sun until 6pm; admission fee) on Leopold de Waelplaats. The fine collection of Flemish art covers five centuries, with the master Rubens being well represented – his works include *Adoration of the Magi* and *St Francis of Assisi*. There are also many paintings by the Rubens school and Rubens' illustrious pupils, including Antoon van Dyck and Jacob Jordaens. Hans Memling, Dirk Bouts and another Antwerp master, Quentin Massys, also have works here. A collection of beautiful art of the Rubens school can also be found in **Sint-Pauluskerk** (St Paul's Church) on Sint-Paulusstraat. The church was part of a Dominican monastery and was constructed during the mid-16th century in the late-Gothic style. The interior is decorated with fine wood panelling surpassed only by the majesty of 15 large canvasses depicting the *Mysteries of the Rosaries*, painted by 11 different master painters.

Rubens House

The **Rubenshuis** (Rubens House; open Tues–Sun 10am–5pm; admission fee) at Wapper 9–11, located just off the main shopping street, Meir, is today surrounded by modern shops and cafés, although it still gives an impression of the immense wealth and influence of arguably the best- known Belgian artist. He used the money earned from painting portraits of European royalty to build a large and substantial home for his family – eight children by two wives – and a studio for himself in 1610. He must have been happy with the result, as he spent the last 30 years of his life here. The family lived in a Flemish-style wing of the house. It is austerely furnished, but look out for a self-portrait of the

Street performer

Inside Antwerp's Sint-Carolus Borromeuskerk

artist hanging in the dining room. Contrast this family wing with the studio, which was decorated in the then-fashionable Baroque style. Here you will find Rubens' extensive collection of Greek and Roman sculpture.

Rubens had a hand in the design and adornment of the early 17th-century **Sint-Carolus Borromeuskerk** (St Charles Borromeo Church; open Mon–Sat 10am–12.30pm and 2–5pm; admission fee), set in Hendrik Conscienceplein, east of the Grote Markt. The artist, along with members of his family, is buried in the **Sint-Jacobskerk** (St James's Church), inside which there are a number of his paintings, and a portrait of Rubens.

Works by Rubens are also in evidence in the **Mayer Van den Bergh Museum** (open Tues–Sun 10am–5pm; admission fee) on Lange Gasthuisstraat, and although Pieter Bruegel was a native of Brussels, there are several of his works here, including his earliest known painting, *Twelve Proverbs,* and his pessimistic view of war *Dulle Griet* (Mad Meg). The museum is based on the private collection of Sir Fritz van den Bergh and includes a large collection of sculpture, tapestries, and ceramics from the 12th to the 18th centuries, in addition to a wide range of art.

Museum of Modern Art

Known as MUHKA, the **Museum voor Hedendaagse Kunst Antwerpen** (Antwerp Museum of Modern Art; open Tues–Sun 10am–5pm; admission fee) occupies a former warehouse in Antwerp's old port, on Leuvenstraat, close to the Scheldt. Behind the warehouse's original Art Deco façade, a collection of cutting-edge Belgian and international art is expanding to fill the enormous interior.

In the newer part of town (c.19th century) across the ring road, a wide boulevard skirts the old town. Browse in the modern stores lining Meir, a pedestrian-only area. As Meir becomes Leystraat, the buildings take on a fabulously ornate style, flanking Teniersplein with its statue of the artist David Tenier (a relative of Bruegel). Cross Frankrijklei and walk towards the railway station along Keyserlei. To your left is **De Vlaamse Opera** (Flemish Opera House), designed in 1907.

Diamonds Galore

To the right of Keyserlei is the diamond district where 70 percent of the world's raw diamonds come to be graded, polished and set. This weighs in at 25 million carats each year. The streets here are filled with jewellery shops selling items from only a few euros to individual pieces worth hundreds of thousands. If you want to know more about this most precious of minerals, head to Diamondland in Appelmansstraat. This diamond showroom and polishing house features films and polishing exhibitions about the trade.

In the neighbourhood of Antwerp Centraal Station is the **Diamantkwartier** (Diamond Quarter), the centre of the city's diamond trade. The collection of the **Diamantmuseum Provincie Antwerpen** (Antwerp Province Diamond Museum; open May–Oct daily 10am–6pm; Nov–Dec and Feb–Apr 10am–5pm; free) on Koningin Astridplein includes a reproduction of the Cullinan diamond, the largest ever found, from South Africa.

Antwerp Station was designed in French Renaissance style and opened in 1905. Its fine dome is reminiscent of a cathedral, and the station's fine proportions bear testament to the importance of investment in the rail industry at the end of the 19th century.

Beyond the station is **Antwerp Zoo** (open daily 9am–dusk; admission fee), founded in 1843 on 10 hectares (247 acres) of land. It was an extremely important collection at that time and has remained at the forefront of developments both in animal welfare and research into endangered species.

Bruges

This small Belgian city, known as Brugge in Dutch, was one of the most influential in northern Europe, with a thriving economy in the Middle Ages based on trade with Europe and England. It was the leading city for textile and tapestry production and was a major trading town of the Hanseatic League. Cargoes of wool, furs and spices passed through its port, which was connected to the sea via the Zwin inlet. In 1384, the Burgundian leader Philip the Good made Bruges the capital of his growing kingdom, and artists Hans Memling and Jan van Eyck were at

> A tour through the canals of Bruges in an open boat is a delightful experience, and the view from this splendid vantage-point is memorable. All boats cover the same route and depart from several landing stages around the centre (Mar–Nov 10am–6pm; tour fee).

the centre of a royal court that was one of the most splendid in Europe. However, the city lost its influence as early as the 15th century. Cheap textile imports from England flooded the market, and the River Zwin began to silt up. Bruges became land-locked and in time was forgotten.

However, it was this sudden loss of prestige and influence that has helped to make Bruges one of Europe's most popular tourist destinations. The town was never redeveloped, and today it still has an almost complete historical area dating from the early 16th century. Most of its canals remain, and a stroll along the narrow streets offers picture-perfect views.

Tours by Carriage and Boat

Bruges is eminently walkable, but before you start your own exertions take a tour of the streets by horse-drawn carriage or along the small network of canals by boat. If you have the

View from Rozenhoedkaai, in Bruges, across to the Belfry

A ride around Bruges

time, try both, as they offer contrasting experiences in different parts of town.

The Markt

Bruges has two town squares, which are linked by a short street (Breidelstraat). The **Markt** is the larger of the two, and the commercial centre of the town. In the middle of the square is a 19th-century statue, a tribute to the leaders of a 1302 revolt against French overlords. On the southeast side of the square is the **Belfort-Hallen** (Belfry and Covered Market; Tues–Sun 9.30am–5pm; Covered Market free; admission fee for Belfry), built in the 13th century. The belfry was built at the same time, but extended, and the clock was added in the 15th century. Climb to the top, 366 steps and 84m (276ft) up, for a panoramic view over the pitched red roofs and chimneystacks below. Part of the way up around the steep stairwell, you pass the impressive 47-bell carillon. Inside the Belfry was the town treasury, and such were the riches of the town that they could only be accessed with nine separate keys. The Markt was once served by a canal that brought goods directly to the market hall. The adjacent 19th-century neo-Gothic **Provinciaal Hof** (Provincial Palace) is the seat of the West Flanders provincial government.

The Burg and Town Hall

The **Burg** is the smaller of the two squares, and the oldest, dating back to medieval times. It was named after the original castle of Bruges (no longer standing). Each building on the Burg reveals its own beauty, and together, they make one of the most coherent, sequential architectural statements in Europe. On the south side of the square is the **Stadhuis** (Town Hall; Tues–Sun 9.30am–5pm; admission fee), a Gothic masterpiece built from 1376 to 1420. Its façade is incredibly ornate with a wealth of fascinating detail, adorned with statues of the counts of Flanders, family crests and scenes of daily medieval life. Inside, there is even more evidence of civic pride, with guild pennants hanging from the ceiling. The Gothic Hall on the second floor has a magnificent vaulted wooden ceiling decorated with gilt. The whole building was completely renovated in the mid-1990s.

The Belfry is the dominant landmark of Bruges

To the right of the Stadhuis is the **Landhuis van het Brugse Vrije** (the Palace of the Liberty of Bruges). The mansion is an interesting amalgam of architectural styles. It is renowned for its ornate chimneypiece of marble, alabaster and oak, dating from 1531, in the **Renaissancezaal van het Brugse Vrije** (Renaissance Hall of the Liberty of Bruges; open Tues–Sun 9.30am–5pm, also Easter Mon, Pentecost Mon; admission fee). At its centre is a statue of Charles V in full ceremonial armour, surrounded by other members of

Gilded statue in the Heilig-Bloed-basiliek (Basilica of the Holy Blood)

the Habsburg dynasty. At the rear of the complex are the remains of a 16th-century structure that housed the Law Courts. The façade in front of the square is 18th century. Here you will find the Bruges Tourist Office. Between the Stadhuis and Tourist Office is the **Oude Civiele Griffie** (Old Recorders House), completed in 1537.

Basilica of the Holy Blood

West of the Stadhuis, in the darkest corner of the square, is the small entrance to the most important religious building in the city. This is the **Heilig-Bloedbasiliek** (Basilica of the Holy Blood; open Apr–Sept daily 9.30am–noon and 2–6pm; Oct–Mar Thur–Tues 10am–noon and 2–4pm, Wed 10am–noon; church free; admission fee to treasury), whose façade was completed in 1534.

Inside, there are two small and richly decorated chapels. The lower chapel is 12th-century Romanesque, while the upper one is 16th-century Gothic in style, with 19th-century alterations. It is in a side room of this upper chapel that the relic that gives the basilica its name is kept. When the Flemish knight Dirk of Alsace returned in 1150 from the Second Crusade, he brought back a phial containing what he alleged was a drop of Christ's blood. The blood was said to have turned liquid on several occasions, and this was declared miraculous by Pope Clement V. Bruges became a centre of pilgrimage for people wishing to worship at the chapel.

In 1611, the archdukes of Spain presented the church with an ornate silver tabernacle in which the phial is now stored. In the early days, the phial was displayed publicly on a weekly basis. Today, it only leaves the side chapel once per year on Ascension Day in May, when it is carried through the streets of Bruges in one of the most elaborate processions in Belgium. The gold-and-silver reliquary used to transport the phial can be seen in a small treasury just off the chapel. Opposite the Stadhuis, near the basilica, is the **Proosdij**, formerly the palace of the bishops of Bruges.

Rozenhoedkaai and Huidenvettersplein

Take the route through the narrow archway between the Stadhuis and the Oude Civiele Griffie. You'll cross one of Bruges's network of canals and see the covered fish market (**Vismarkt**) just ahead. A walk to the left would take you along some beautiful streets. However, continuing on to the right leads you to several important attractions. Have your camera at the ready for some archetypal views of the town from Rozenhoedkaai.

On the diminutive square of **Huidenvettersplein,** several small houses are huddled at the water's edge, with the belfry rising gracefully behind and weeping willows softening the red brick. When the tour boats pass on **Groenerei** (Green Canal), you can hardly fail to be enchanted. Keep an eye out for the **Pelikaanhuis**

Fish market motif

(Pelican House), easily identified by the emblem of the bird above the door. Built in 1634, this was one of many almshouses in the city. There are several boarding points for water trips along the canal-side here, though you may have to queue.

Museum of Fine Arts

The street of Dijver runs alongside Groenerei. Here you will find several major museums. First is the **Groeninge Museum** (Museum of Fine Arts; open Tues–Sun 9.30am–5pm, also Easter Mon, Pentecost Mon; admission fee), which displays a fine collection of Flemish masters including the work of Jan Van Eyck, particularly his *Madonna with Canon George Van der Paele*, of Hieronymus Bosch and Gerard David. Works of later artists such as René Magritte are also on display. Take a walk around the gardens. The

---

Flemish Masters

A group of early Flemish artists, based mostly in Bruges and Ghent, have had their work handed down to us under the banner of the 'Flemish Primitives'. Yet the luminous, revolutionary work of Jan van Eyck (1385–1441), whose *Adoration of the Mystic Lamb* is in Ghent's St Bavo's Cathedral, can scarcely be thought of as primitive. Nor can that of his contemporaries Rogier van der Weyden (*c.*1399–1464), Hans Memling (*c.*1430–94) and Petrus Christus (*c.*1410–72), who shared Van Eyck's fondness for realistic portrayals of human and natural subjects.

Later, the focus of attention switched to Antwerp and, to a lesser degree, to Brussels. The occasionally gruesome works of Pieter Brueghel the Elder (1525–69), the sensuous paintings of Peter Paul Rubens (1577–1640) and the output of Rubens's students Jacob Jordaens (1593–1678) and Antoon van Dyck (1599–1641) cemented the Flemish connection with the finest art of its day.

whole vista is typically Flemish, with its low-rise, cottage-style white buildings with red tile roofs.

Nearby is the **Brangwyn Museum** (open Tues–Sun 9.30am–5pm, also Easter Mon, Pentecost Mon; admission fee), featuring the extensive collection of Arts and Crafts exponent Sir Frank Brangwyn, who was born in Bruges and bequeathed his work and col-

Four Horsemen of the Apocalypse by Rik Poot

lection to the city when he died in 1956. As a student of William Morris, Brangwyn is an important link to later artistic movements, and his work is a contrast to the earlier Flemish masters that are so abundant across the city.

The **Gruuthuse Museum** (open Tues–Sun 9.30am–5pm, also Easter Mon, Pentecost Mon; admission fee), so called because the original owners had the right to tax the *'gruut'*, the basic mash of herbs, barley and plants used in the brewing process, is next.

The building housing the museum is itself worth seeing. Erected in the 15th century, it has twice housed fugitive English kings – Henry IV in 1471, and Charles II in 1656. In the garden, a romantic brick bridge crosses one of Bruges's narrower canals, offering yet another picture opportunity. You will also find Rik Poot's sculpture-group, *Four Horsemen of the Apocalypse,* gracing the outer courtyard.

The rooms of the mansion display a wealth of daily articles including furniture and utensils. The huge kitchen is particularly interesting – it looks as if the 15th-century cook has just stepped out of it to do the daily shopping.

The tomb of Mary of Burgundy in the Church of Our Lady

At the end of Dijver is the **Onze-Lieve-Vrouwekerk** (Church of Our Lady; open Mon–Fri 9am–12.30pm and 1.30–5pm, Sat 9am–12.30pm and 1.30–4pm, Sun 1.30–5pm; church free; admission fee to sanctuary of Charles and Mary and museum), an imposing church that has a 122-m (400-ft) brick tower – the second highest in Belgium, after Antwerp Cathedral's. Inside the church you will find the gilded tombs of Charles the Bold and his daughter Mary of Burgundy, whose premature death at the age of 25 brought the Burgundian period of Belgian history to an end. Our Lady's also displays a sculpture of the *Madonna and Child* by Michelangelo, the only one to be exported from Italy during the artist's lifetime.

Hans Memling Museum

Situated opposite the entrance to the church, through an archway, is the **Sint-Janshospitaal** (St John's Hospital). Dating from the 12th century, it is the oldest building in Bruges. It remained in use until the 19th century. In the old hospital church you will find the **Memlingmuseum** (open Tues–Sun 9.30am–5pm, also Easter Mon, Pentecost Mon; admission fee), which is devoted to the work of the German-born master Hans Memling. Although the collection is not extensive, each piece is a particularly fine example. Look for the *Mystic Marriage of St Ursula*; the exquisite detail of this painting makes it one of Belgium's national treasures. The hospital complex also has a pleasant bar/

brasserie with a sun terrace, making it an ideal place to take a break.

Walk south down Mariastraat with its selection of chocolate and lace shops. A left turn at Wijngardstraat leads to the Bejginhof, but before this, look for the small square of Walplein and **De Halve Maan Brewery** (open for guided tours Apr–Sept daily, hourly 10am–5pm; Oct–Mar daily, 11am and 3pm; admission fee), which has been in operation in the city since 1546. A tour of the present brewery, opened in 1856, takes around 45 minutes, and ends with a taste of the delicious Straffe Hendrik beer.

The Begijnhof

The **Begijnhof** at Bruges was founded in 1245 by Margaret of Constantinople and was active in providing security for lost and abandoned women until the 20th century. The circular collection of white painted buildings dating from the 17th century – an oasis of solitude even in quiet Bruges – is now home to a community of the Benedictine order. Please respect their request for peace and quiet as you walk through the gardens. Just before the main entrance is an open area with a pretty canal and a range of restaurants. The horse-drawn carriages turn around

St John's Hospital, the oldest building in Bruges

Bear at the Burghers' Lodge

here on their tours. You'll find a water fountain here for them, decorated with a horse's head.

From the fountain, it is only a couple of minutes walk to the **Minnewater** (Lake of Love) and a picturesque park. Minnewater was originally the inner harbour of Bruges, before the outlet to the sea silted up. Today, you can see the 15th-century gunpowder house and scant remains of a protective wall. You'll find people cycling and jogging along the path here. The open water is a haven for birds, including swans.

The Old Quaysides

The main canal that served the centre of the old town entered from the north. Today this terminates at **Jan van Eyckplein**, with a statue of the artist, just a couple of minutes away from the Markt. In the square, you can still find fine buildings lining what were once the busy quaysides of Speigelrei and Spinolarei. The 15th-century **Oud Tolhuis** (Old Toll House) is where taxes on goods entering and leaving the city were collected. Today it is home to the city library. Nearby is the **Poorters Loge** (Burghers' Lodge), a kind of gentlemen's club for the wealthy businessmen of Bruges' golden age.

Located in Peperstraat, east of the central canal, is the **Kantcentrum** (Lace Centre; open Mon–Fri 10am–noon and 2–6pm, Sat 10am–noon and 2–5pm; admission fee), a museum and workshop in the 15th-century Jeruzalemgodshuizen (Jerusalem Almshouses). Fine examples of the craft of lace-making, and demonstrations by lacemakers, can be seen.

Ghent

In the 12th century, Ghent (Gent in Dutch and Gand in French) was one of the largest cities in Europe, thriving on its trade in textiles and its position at the confluence of the Leie and Scheldt rivers. Its people were independent and self-assertive; the pagan population threw Christian clergymen into the River Scheldt in 610, and in 1337 they rose up against French rule. Today, it is thriving as a modern commercial town. Thanks to its university, it has a young population, which gives it a vibrancy not felt in Bruges. Ghent also has some interesting historic attractions to enjoy, many of which underwent an extensive period of restoration during the latter

Spires of Ghent from Sint-Michielsbrug (St Michael's Bridge)

part of the 20th century. Much of the town centre is traffic-free, except for the tram services, which adds to the enjoyment of walking. Perhaps the best place to start your tour is at **Sint-Michielsbrug** (St Michael's Bridge), spanning the River Leie to the west of the old town. To the left are the old quaysides of Graslei and Korenlei, and beyond them is the medieval castle of Gravensteen. Three of Ghent's landmarks – Sint-Niklaaskerk, Belfort and Sint-Baafskathedraal – lie ahead.

The Church of St Nicholas

The church of **Sint-Niklaas** (St Nicholas) was built from the 13th to the 18th centuries and is hence an amalgam of architectural styles. Beyond the church is the **Belfort** (Belfry; open daily mid-Mar–Apr and Oct–mid-Nov 10am–1pm; Easter and May–Sept 10am–1pm and 2–6pm; admission fee), completed in 1380. A recent refurbishment has re-gilded the clock-face, and the dragon that sits atop the spire. In summer, you can take a lift to the viewing platform 91m (298ft) above the town, for tremendous views.

Ghent's Sint-Baafskathedraal

Nearby is the **Lakenhalle** (Cloth Hall), a symbol of corporate power when it was completed in 1441. Both the Belfort and Lakenhalle are on Botermarkt (Butter Market), one of the major meeting places in centuries gone by.

In the 16th century, it was decided to build the new **Stadhuis** (Town Hall; guided tours only, reserved in advance; admission fee) on the north side of the square. Like Sint-Niklaaskerk, the Stadhuis took many decades to complete. Work was halted in 1639 and only recommenced as the 18th century dawned. By this time a new architectural style was in

Ghent Altarpiece by Jan van Eyck

vogue. You will notice that the building has one Renaissance façade facing Botermarkt, a Baroque one opposite Hoogpoort and a Rococo façade on the Poeljemarkt side. In summer there are guided tours of the ornate interior; they include the magnificent **Pacificatiezaal** (Pacification Room), where the Pacification of Ghent, a treaty aimed (fruitlessly) at ending the religious wars in the Low Countries, was signed in 1576.

St Bavo's Cathedral

The third spire to be seen from Sint-Michielsbrug is that of **Sint-Baafskathedraal** (St Bavo's Cathedral; open Apr–Oct daily 8.30am–6pm; Nov–Mar daily 8.30am–5pm; cathedral free; admission fee to crypt and *Mystic Lamb* chapel). This imposing granite-and-brick edifice is also a mixture of styles, with a chancel dating from the 14th century, a nave from the 15th century and a transept from the 16th century.

The art inside the cathedral represents some of Belgium's greatest cultural treasures. To the left of the main entrance is a small chapel containing what has become known as the *Ghent Altarpiece*, a Jan van Eyck masterpiece called *The Adoration of the Mystic Lamb*. Here, Van Eyck achieved reality through painstaking attention to every detail, breaking away from the medieval stylised form. Other masterpieces include *The Conversion of St Bavo* by Rubens and a work by Frans Pourbus, *Christ Amongst the Doctors*, which has many luminaries of the time painted as onlookers in the crowd.

Korenlei and Graslei

Just to the left of Sint-Michielsbrug, **Korenlei** and **Graslei** once formed the main harbour of Ghent, known as Tussen Bruggen (Between the Bridges). Here you can find some of Ghent's finest old buildings, guild houses and warehouses. Both sides of the river are equally beautiful, but on Graslei, look out particularly for the **Gildehuis van de Vrije Schippers** (House of the Free Boatmen), built in 1531, and Het Spijker (1200), which has been tastefully developed into a bar and eatery. Korenlei rivals its neighbour with **Gildehuis van de Onvrije Schippers** (House of the Tied Boatmen), a Flemish Baroque masterpiece dating from 1739, and De Zwane, a former brewery of the 16th century.

Gravensteen Castle

Walk north along the river, and as it splits, you will see the grey walls of **Gravensteen Castle** (open Apr–Sept daily 9am–6pm; Oct–Mar daily 9am–5pm; admission fee) ahead. The outline that Gravensteen presents is the stuff of fairytales: crenellations and turrets, tiny slits for archers to fire their arrows, and a moat to stop invaders. The castle was the seat for the counts of the region and from its construction in 1180 it represented their huge power and wealth. Inside you can visit their living quarters, the torture chamber and dungeons, where grisly instruments are on view.

Just west of the Leie, the **Design Museum Gent** (open Tues–Sun 10am–6pm; admission fee) occupies a graceful mansion from 1755 with a central courtyard. The rooms display interior design and furnishings up to the 19th century. A separate wing contains modern furniture.

The Patershol

Behind the Gravensteen, the **Patershol** district is a jumble of narrow medieval streets, dotted with restaurants and cafés. A short walk leads to the city's folklore museum, **Het Huis van Alijn** (Alijn House; open Tues–Sun 11am–5pm; admission fee). The museum collection includes numerous everyday articles for spinning and weaving, animal husbandry and cooking, and is housed in a series of almshouses dating from 1363.

Colourful façades and reflections along Ghent's attractive Korenlei

Vridagmarkt still holds its Friday market, but visitors arrive to view Dulle Griet or Mad Meg at other times of the week. This is the huge 16-ton cannon, which stands on the nearby quayside. There are numerous pretty houses on the square, including Ons Huis, built in 1900.

Art lovers should not miss the **Museum voor Schone Kunsten** (Museum of Fine Arts; open Tues–Sun 10am–6pm; admission fee) in Citadelpark. Works include examples by Frans Hals, Pieter Breughel the Younger, Rubens and Bosch. The **Stedelijk Museum voor Actuele Kunst** (SMAK; Museum of Modern Art; open Tues–Sun 10am–6pm; admission fee) opposite offers a collection of different 20th-century Belgian artists.

WHAT TO DO

In addition to hundreds of things to see, Brussels also has lots to do, with several important performance venues, a plethora of bars and some delightful shopping opportunities.

SHOPPING

Though there are no 'zones' as such, certain districts do have a greater density of certain speciality shops. The streets around the Grand-Place are filled with shops selling cheap knick-knacks, T-shirts, mugs and keyrings – all the usual budget remembrances. For antiques head towards the Sablon area, where there are also some excellent art galleries. The weekend market in place du Grand-Sablon has some interesting items. For the antiques of tomorrow, head to the flea market at place du Jeu-de-Balle in the Marolles – a veritable treasure trove of memorabilia, furniture, porcelain and glasswear. For books, try Galerie Bortier, uphill from the Grand-Place, whose stores have a huge collection.

For haute couture, visit Avenue Louise, the nearby Porte de Namur and the several galleries in between, where fine boutiques and department stores are full of the best European fashions and also feature Belgian designers. For a selection of high fashion in the centre of town, visit the **Galeries Royales St-Hubert**, where Delvaux has its signature store. For modern fashions try the rue Antoine Dansaert, across from the Bourse. Further out, boulevard de Waterloo also has numerous good stores along its length.

High-street fashion and all the best-known European names can be found on the rue Neuve, north of place de la Monnaie. If it's raining, make for the modern shopping malls of Centre Anspach and Centre de la Monnaie. Stamps and coins can be found in numerous shops in the narrow streets around rue du Midi, a few minutes south of the Grand-Place.

What to Buy

With a tradition of trade guilds going back to the Middle Ages, it should not be surprising that Brussels still excels in many crafts. Artistic inspiration takes a number of forms, and as you walk along the city streets, there is sure to be something to catch your eye.

Lace. The women in Brussels' *béguinages* and its ladies of the court spent many hours creating fine lace, which adorned clothing and ceremonial garments.

Making lace in Bruges

Nowadays, this lace is used to decorate handkerchiefs, napkins, table linens and special items such as christening gowns. Prices vary greatly between machine-produced lace and hand-worked items; knowledgeable sales assistants will help by explaining the different qualities of the pieces on display.

Tapestry. Belgium was renowned for its tapestry-making during the reign of the Burgundians and the Habsburgs. The huge tapestries designed for the ruling families incorporated gold and silver thread and were considered so valuable that they were classed as part of the royal treasury. Today, the tradition continues, but, as with lace, much of the tapestry on sale is machine-produced. Handmade work is exquisite, but comes at a high price. You can buy traditional items such as wall coverings or more modern items such as luggage, clothing, or soft home furnishings (cushions and curtains).

Books and Antiques. For many years Brussels sat on a major trading route, and it is clear from the range of items available in antique and antiquarian bookshops that goods found their way to Belgium from all across Europe, and later, the colonies. Furniture from England and France sits alongside glass from the Habsburg Empire of Eastern Europe. Prices are steep, but the level of expertise in stores around place du Grand-Sablon is equally high.

Silver and Jewellery. Jewellers to the royal court produced beautiful pieces, and today's gold- and silversmiths continue in the same fashion.

Art. A number of commercial galleries feature the work of established artists and newcomers in a range of genres. Pop art is particularly popular at present, but it is by no means monopolising the arena. You can also buy original cartoon fiches from the heroes of the celluloid screen, such as Hergé's *Tintin*. A good starting point is the Comic Strip Centre in rue de Sables *(see page 39)*, but there's also the Tintin Shop at rue de la Colline 13.

Stamps and Coins. A collection of the world's stamps and coins can be found in small dusty shops around the city. There

Lace Society

Belgium has a tradition of making lace – a threadwork of silk, linen or cotton – that stretches back to the 16th century in Flanders. Brussels and Bruges are the principal sales points. Beware of cheap machine-made and imported imitations, unless you only want a simple souvenir. Belgian handmade lace is expensive, but if you like lace this is the only sort worth buying. It should always be purchased from a reputable shop and clearly labelled as having been handmade in Belgium.

may be something for your collection here, or you can sell/ swap your stamps.

Delvaux Handbags. These have been at the height of Belgian fashion for many years. Their simple lines and excellent construction have made them very popular among well-heeled, stylish women in Europe.

Edibles. The delightful chocolate and pralines produced in Belgium are available all across town in pretty presentation boxes for you to take home. Dandoy has been producing *speculoos* biscuits for several generations; you'll find their shop just off the Grand-Place. Alternatively, try Marcolini chocolates. These are hand-produced and absolutely delicious. Beer is, of course, another option. With hundreds of different types to choose from, you'll need to do some thorough research before making your choice. Many off-licences have selections of beer ready for you to take home.

Hats off to Belgium's stallholders

ENTERTAINMENT

As Belgium is a small country, it welcomes foreign companies in the performing arts. With more than 30 venues in the city, there will be a wealth of performances taking place whatever time of year you visit.

Rich and delicious Belgian chocolates galore

The galleries of Brussels hold a huge number of temporary exhibitions of art from around the world. All the arts are represented, including many new art forms such as video and internet art. The Brussels International Tourist Office in the Grand-Place produces a seasonal pamphlet with details of exhibitions that are taking place while you are in the city.

Theatre and Music

When the museums close at night, Brussels takes on a different character. There are several prominent theatre companies around the city, including the **Théâtre Royal de la Monnaie** (place de la Monnaie; tel: 02-229 1200), where the seeds of the 'Belgian revolution' were sown in 1830. It continues to be a major venue, with a programme of opera and ballet. The **Théâtre National de la Communauté Wallonie Bruxelles** (boulevard Emile Jacqmain 111-115; tel: 02-203 4155) was founded in 1945 and produces strong performances. **Théâtre de la Place des Martyrs** (tel: 02-223 3208), is a converted cinema that is home to the Théâtre en Liberté Company. For a light-hearted view of theatre, try the **Théâtre Royal de Toone** (Impasse Schud-

Inside the Théâtre Royal de la Monnaie

develd, Petite rue des Bouchers 21; tel: 02-217 2723), a puppet theatre that has been operated by the same family since 1830. They perform classical plays and local folk tales with marionettes.

Classical music venues in Brussels include the glasshouses of **Le Botanique** (rue Royale 236; tel: 02-218 3732) and the **Palais des Beaux-Arts** (rue Ravenstein 23; tel: 02-507 8200), which is fashionably known as **Bozar**, and which hosts the Queen Elisabeth Music Competition (held on three out of every four years), as well as numerous concerts. The largest concert hall is **Forest National** south of the city, with an 8,000-seat capacity (tel: 02-340 2211; tram 18 or 52). Here, you'll be able to see pop concerts by many international names. For up-and-coming performers, try the **Ancienne Belgique** (boulevard Anspach 110; tel: 02-548 2424); everyone from Edith Piaf to the Clash has played here.

Nightlife

Nightclubs are numerous and popular in Brussels, and each one has a different character. Entrance policies can be strict, and if your 'look' doesn't fit you may not be allowed in, so be sure to dress accordingly. Most open around 11pm and don't close until the early morning. Two of the best for visitors are **Le Sud** (rue de l'Ecuyer 43), a café/bar/nightclub frequented by clients of all ages, and **L'Espace de Nuit Capitale** (rue du Marché-aux-Fromages 10), a large club just off the Grand-Place.

For cinemas, there are two complexes that show English-speaking films with French/Dutch subtitles. UGC (place Brouckère; tel: 0900-10440), has eight screens showing the latest Hollywood releases; **Kinepolis** at Bruparck (tel: 0900-00555), is a 26-screen complex with a 600-sq-m IMAX screen for visual spectaculars. The **Musée du Cinema** (rue Baron Horta 9; tel: 02-507 8370) screens classic 'talkies' and silent movies every day.

Perhaps the most 'Belgian' thing to do in the evenings is to enjoy one of the hundreds of different beers that this country produces, and take a while to get into conversation with one of the locals or one of the thousands of fellow visitors from around the world.

FESTIVALS

Belgium has a number of festivals that have their antecedents in the Middle Ages – a Golden Age for many towns. Brussels holds the **Ommegang** early in July each year. Originally it had a religious significance, but it soon came to celebrate the power of the old trade corporations in the city. Today's festival commemorates the time in 1549 when the guilds and Chambers of Rhetoric, as they were called, paraded their pennants before Emperor Charles V. The Ommegang fell into disuse, but was revived in 1930. Today the modern bearers of

Flower market on the Grand-Place

the head of the guilds dress in costumes of the mid-1500s and carry the banners and pennants of their trades around the Grand-Place.

The **Carpet of Flowers** is a biennial celebration held in mid-August in the Grand-Place, when a huge elaborate tapestry of begonias almost fills the square.

Bruges' greatest festivity takes place usually in the latter part of May each year, when the whole town comes out to witness the **Procession of the Holy Blood** (*Heilig-Bloedprocessie*). At this time, the most holy relic of the cathedral, said to contain a drop of Christ's blood, is paraded around the city. Solemn religious services are held across the city before the merrymaking begins.

SPORTS

With over 30 sq m (320 sq ft) of green space for each resident of Brussels, and a surrounding landscape without any appreciable hills, it is easy to understand why sports are a big part of the city's life.

Cycling. This is a popular sport, though not in the centre of Brussels, where there are a number of deceptive inclines to watch out for (to say nothing of the dangerous traffic conditions). In the suburbs and through the forests there are cycle routes and most urban areas have cycle lanes. It is easy to rent bikes – many railway stations have a bike hire office. Don't forget to wear a cycling helmet.

Football. This is a passion in Belgium, as in most other European countries. Sporting Club de Anderlecht is one of the most successful teams, with several international wins. For details, contact the stadium at avenue Théo Verbeek 2, Anderlecht (tel: 02-522 1539). The season runs from September to May. The National Stadium (Stade Roi Baudouin) is at Heysel. It holds international games, cup finals, and other national sporting events (tel: 02-479 3654).

Horse-Riding. The forests and woods have bridleways for horse-riding.

Jogging and Running. Both are popular, and you are sure to see people taking a turn around the parks. A 20-km (12-mile) road race takes place in May with a huge number of local entrants, and there's the Brussels Marathon in September.

Leisure Centres. Because the weather in Belgium is often inclement, there are a number of covered sports complexes around the city. The Centre Sportif de Woluwe-Saint-Pierre, rue Salomé 2 (tel: 02-773 1820), has squash, outdoor and indoor tennis, a swimming pool, sauna and Turkish bath.

Walking. The leafy Forêt de Soignes is the perfect place for forgetting the city and surrounding yourself with birdsong. There are marked routes for walkers.

Forêt de Soignes

Water Sports. Everything from rowing or pedalo rides on local lakes, to water-skiing and windsurfing is available. Visit the lakes at Tervuren, Bois de la Cambre and Forêt de Soignes.

BRUSSELS FOR CHILDREN

At first glance, Brussels may not be the best place to take children. However, the city reveals some interesting and entertaining things that are bound to keep your children happy. Carriage rides are great fun, allowing children to rise above the sea of heads for a better view. These take place in Brussels and Antwerp during the summer, and in Bruges all year round. You can take a canal or river cruise in Antwerp, Bruges and Ghent.

The **Bruparck** complex has several different attractions. **L'Océade** offers water sports, rides and pools – great on a hot summer day. **Mini-Europe** is the 'child-size' attraction, and is both fun and educational. The eruption of Vesuvius is probably the most popular, with its ground-shaking power.

Many of Brussels' museums have fun and educational attractions that are specifically designed with children in mind. The **Scientastic Centre** in the Bourse métro station has simple, hands-on experiments and 'magic' tricks, and the **Natural Sciences Museum**, with its dinosaurs to enthrall young imaginations, also has special activities and workshops for children aged 4–12 years. The Dynamuseum in the **Cinquantenaire Museum** complex offers special activities for children aged 6–12 years, and the **Musical Instruments Museum** offers multi-sensory experimentation with sound, along with training courses and workshops.

There is a **Children's Museum** at rue de Bourgmestre 15 (tel: 02-640 0107) that operates a regular programme of sessions involving painting, collage, woodworking and theatre for young children. The **Théâtre Royal de Toone** (tel: 02-217 2723) puppet theatre in Petite rue des Bouchers has live performances throughout the year. For other children's theatre performances, contact the **Information Centre for Young People's Theatre** (tel: 02-648 3458). Many activities specifically for children are conducted in French and Dutch. For details of programmes in English, contact each organisation directly.

Castles always spark the imagination and **Gravensteen Castle** in Ghent is no exception. Images of sword fights on the battlements and prisoners in the dungeons flash through the mind.

The parks and forests provide perfect environments in which to walk, cycle or ride. The lake at **Tervuren** has boats for hire. If you prefer something more relaxing, take a rug and a picnic and just enjoy the sunshine; don't forget to take some bread to feed the ducks and geese.

Open space at the Atomium, a giant model of an iron crystal

If you and your family really need a break from the city, then try the **Walibi** and **Aqualibi**, situated only 19km (12 miles) southeast of Brussels. This huge theme park has a number of mechanical rides with spirals, catapults, river rapids and an attraction entitled *1,001 Arabian Nights*. Aqualibi water park has cascades, whirlpools and jungle experiences. There are numerous opportunities for refreshment, so you can spend the whole day here. (To reach the theme park by car, take the E411 and leave at the Brussels Namur exit; by train, take the Ottignies/Louvain-la-Neuve line, get off at Bierges station, only 300m (330yds) from the park entrance.)

Calendar of Events

Brussels holds numerous annual events throughout the year. Many of these happen around the same time every year, but exact dates are subject to change, so check with the Brussels National Tourist Office *(see page 128)* before planning a trip around one of these events.

January Brussels International Film Festival.

February Mardi Gras, carnival parades.

April Baroque Spring in the Sablon, classical music performances. The Queen Elisabeth International Music Competition (held on three out of four years). Floraliën of Ghent, international flower show.

April–May Royal Greenhouses *(Serres)* at Laeken are open to the public.

April–October Festival of Flanders, classical music events in abbeys, cathedrals and city halls throughout Flanders.

May Brussels International Arts Festival: two weeks of dance, theatre and opera performances at venues throughout the city. Museums day: on one day in May many Brussels museums offer free entrance.

Late-May Procession of the Holy Blood in Bruges. Brussels Jazz Marathon, an international jazz festival with venues around the city.

June Brussels open-air music festival in the city's squares and parks.

June–August A light-and-sound show in the Grand-Place.

June–October Festival of Wallonia, classical musical events in Wallonia.

July Ommegang procession on the first Tuesday and Thursday of the month. Belgium's National Day, 21 July: fireworks at the place des Palais. Ghent Festivities, a medieval fair and street entertainment.

July–September The Palais Royal is open to the public.

August Canal Festival, Bruges.

9 August Planting of the Maypole.

15 August Every two years on this day, a flower carpet is laid out on the Grand-Place.

September Brussels Marathon. Antwerp's Feast of Liberation and Festival of the Guilds.

December Unveiling of the Christmas crib and lights in the Grand-Place, where there is a Christmas market and ice-skating rink.

EATING OUT

Brussels has no shortage of fine restaurants, and its people enjoy eating out. City chefs have added personal twists to the national dishes of their neighbours to produce their own delicious and unique creations. However, Belgium does not have to look abroad for good food. It has a fine national and regional cuisine of its own, with hearty dishes based on fresh local ingredients. There are numerous eateries from formal to informal, with a range of prices, so you should find something to match your taste and budget.

As a cosmopolitan city, Brussels has some excellent international restaurants offering French, Chinese, Vietnamese, Greek, Moroccan and Japanese cuisine, among others. However, if you want to try Belgian cuisine, the following information will help you through the menu.

Some Brussels restaurants are happy to allow diners' dogs into the dining room, and many let them on to outside terraces. Smoking is still very popular here, which sometimes affects the quality of the air in bars and restaurants.

WHEN TO EAT

French fries make a great snack

Formal eating in Brussels means fitting your appetite into set hours. Few restaurants stay open throughout the day. Lunch (*déjeuner*) takes place between noon and 2.30pm, while dinner (*diner*) is usually from 6pm until around 10.30 or 11pm.

However, don't worry that you won't be able to eat

at all in the afternoon in Brussels. There are numerous informal *brasseries* and cafés that serve delicious food – though perhaps with a simpler menu – throughout the day. Look out for signs saying 'nonstop' outside an establishment, which simply means what it says.

WHAT TO EAT

There is a wide variety of speciality Belgian dishes, both Flemish and Walloon. Many local dishes are seasonal, so which ever time of year you travel, you might not see all those mentioned below on the menu. The best restaurants serving Belgian food will change their menus several times each year to take seasonal offerings into account.

Among hors d'œuvres, there is a beer soup *(soupe à la bière)* with chicken stock and onions; a cold pâté of veal, pork and rabbit known as *potjesvlees; flamiche*, a savoury cheese pie with leeks or onions; *tomate aux crevettes*, tomato filled with shrimp and mayonnaise; and *croquettes de crevette*, small patties of shrimp. Fine smoked ham *(jambon d'Ardenne)* from the forests to the east is also served, thinly sliced with pickles.

Main Dishes

Belgium specialises in stews. The slow-cooked meat is always delicious, the sauce tasty and the vegetables never overcooked. The only 'difficulty' lies in the portions, particularly at the smaller local brasseries, where they tend to be huge.

The best-known main dish is probably *waterzooï*, chicken (or sometimes fish) stewed with whites of leeks, potatoes, bouillon, cream and egg yolks. *Anguille au vert* is eel flavoured with green herbs, usually sorrel, sage and parsley. *Carbonnades flamandes* is a dish consisting of lean beef browned in a pan and then cooked in a casserole with lots of onions and beer. *Pavédes Brasseurs* is a chateaubriand steak with beer sauce. Oxtail (*queue de boeuf*) is also served in a delicious *gueuze* beer sauce (*see box, page 103*). *Hochepot*, a pot-au-feu based on oxtail or pigs' feet, ears and snouts, is another Flemish stew. *Lapin à la flamande* is rabbit marinated in beer and vinegar and braised in onions and prunes. High-quality game usually comes from the Ardennes region to the east, including hare (*lièvre*), venison (*chevreuil*) and pheasant (*faisan*). If you like ham, try *jamboneau*, a shank of ham cooked with cream and served with potatoes and vegetables. *Boudin rouge* is a speciality reminis-

Al fresco on the Grand-Place

cent of blood sausage, while *boudin blanc* is a version of the same, but enlivened by aromatic herbs; both are popular dishes, served with potato purée and an apple compôte.

Vegetables

The Belgian countryside produces top-quality vegetables, and these not only make excellent accompaniments to meat and fish, but also form some extremely delicious main courses in their own right.

Vegetable dishes include *chou rouge à la flamande*, or red cabbage cooked with apples, onions, red wine and vinegar; and *chicon* (braised endives), often served *gratinée au four* (baked with cheese and ham). During the months of April and May, you can find rare delicacies of hop flowers *(jets de houblon)* served with poached eggs and *mousseline* sauce. In spring try *asperges de Malines*, local white asparagus dressed with melted butter and crumbled hard-boiled egg, and *choux de Bruxelles* (Brussels sprouts), often prepared with chestnuts and pieces of bacon, and cooked in goose fat.

Seafood

Even the east of Belgium is only a couple of hours from the sea, so seafood plays a large part in the national cuisine. Most Belgian towns have a fish market that has been in operation for many centuries, and Brussels has long been a big market for retailers and restaurateurs.

Moules (mussels) are probably the most famous Belgian dish. Harvested mostly from nearby Zeeland province in Holland, they are delivered fresh to the capital each morning. Served steaming in a huge bowl, they come with a variety of sauces – *marinières* (white wine and cream), *moutarde* (mustard) and more besides.

One option to try an assortment of fresh seafood, known as an *assiette de fruits de mer* (seafood platter). These dishes may include anything from mussels *(moules)* and spiny lobster *(langoustines)* to oysters *(huîtres)*, crabs *(crabes)*, whelks *(boulots)*, shrimps *(crevettes)* and sea urchins *(oursins)*. Along rue des Bouchers you can watch your plate take shape as a selection is chosen from the display of seafood on ice nearby. Or you could try a fillet or whole fish, delicately

Fish at the market

cooked to preserve its freshness. Try salmon *(saumon)*, sole *(sole)*, bream *(daurade)*, mullet *(rouget)* or sea bass *(loup de mer)*.

Desserts

Most restaurants will offer you cheese as a dessert option. Among as many as 300 different locally produced cheeses are the very strong *remoudou*, the *djotte de Nivelles* and cream cheeses from Brussels.

Crêpes (pancakes) are extremely popular here and are served with a variety of accompaniments. Try them *aux pommes* (with apples) or *à la grecque,* with icing sugar and

Mussels are a Belgian speciality

powdered spices. Or look out for the two-layered pancake with a tasty cheese filling, known as a *double*. Other desserts include *beignets de Bruxelles* (doughnuts or fritters), *tarte au riz* (rice tart), *manons* (chocolates filled with fresh cream) and the famous *speculoos* (spicy gingerbread cut into shapes). Strawberries and other fresh fruit usually appear on restaurant menus all year round, but are best in summer when they are ripened naturally.

For those whose sweet tooth has not been satisfied yet, try fine pralines, local chocolates with delicate fillings of great subtlety both in flavour and variety. Chocolate gateaux take on a spectacular transformation from the ordinary to the divine at the hands of Belgian *chocolatiers*. Belgian chocolates and pralines are exported all over the world, but the best can still be found in Brussels.

Snacks

Waffles *(gaufres)* are the best-known dessert of Belgian origin and these are usually eaten in the street smothered with syrup, or at cafés with a generous helping of chocolate syrup or whipped cream.

If you're looking for a savoury snack to tide you over until the next meal, then try the famous *frites* (French fries), available day and night at special stands *(friteries,* or, in Flemish, *frietekotten)* and usually served in paper cones with salt and mayonnaise. *Caricoles* (sea snails) are another street speciality. Eat them piping hot with the spicy broth in which they were cooked. You will also find a full range of sandwiches on offer. The most popular local bread for sandwiches is the *pistolet,* a small, crusty round roll.

Drinks

Coffee – hot, dark and strong – is the local drink of choice by day. If you want it with milk, ask for it *au lait.* Bars will

The local brew

always serve coffee, tea and hot chocolate in addition to alcoholic drinks, a full range of international-brand spirits plus soft drinks or sodas. Try the local gin, which is known as *pèkèt.*

Most restaurants have a wine list – and some, particularly at the top end of the market, have extremely good cellars – and will offer you a good-value house wine in addition to more expensive bottles. Brasseries and smaller restaurants will also offer house wine in half-litre and litre *pichets* or carafes. These are normally simple, but drinkable wines that pair well with the hearty meals on offer.

Belgian Beer

Belgium is renowned worldwide for its beer. Historically, the cultivation of hops and barley was under the control of the many local monasteries. This resulted in high standards and differing flavours; indeed one particular type of beer, *gueuze*, can only be produced in a small region of the Senne Valley near Brussels because the microorganisms that give the beer its distinct flavour are only found there.

Beer in Belgium is treated with the same degree of reverence as fine wine in France. There are numerous small breweries scattered around the country, producing small quantities of beer for the local market. Each is served in its own style of glass either from the bottle as you watch or from the tap, known as *pression*. Some are extremely high in alcohol content. If you are unsure about which to choose, here is a short introduction to the range of beers you will find on your bar list.

Blanche. A cloudy blond beer made from wheat. Low in alcohol and very refreshing, it is a good option for a sightseeing break.

Brunes. Darker beer.

Lambic. A beer that ferments spontaneously after exposure to the air. Now only produced by smaller independent breweries (a Belgian speciality). Very yeasty in flavour.

Gueuze. A lambic beer that has been allowed to ferment a second time.

Kriek. A lambic beer with the essence of fresh fruit that has been left to develop in huge vats. Cherry is the most popular.

Trappist. This is the strongest beer in Belgium. It is full-flavoured, dark in colour, with a distinctive smell of malt. Trappist beers date from the time of the monasteries and are enjoying a period of renewed popularity today.

To Help You Order...

	French	Dutch
Could we have a table?	**Pouvons-nous avoir une table?**	*Heeft u een tafel voor ons?*
Do you have a set menu?	**Avez-vous un menu du jour?**	*Heeft u een menu van de dag?*
I'd like a/an/some ...	**J'aimerais ...**	*Ik zou graag hebben ...*
beer	**une bière**	*een pils*
butter	**du beurre**	*boter*
bread	**du pain**	*brood*
cheese	**du fromage**	*kaas*
coffee	**un café**	*koffie*
egg(s)	**un (des) œuf(s)**	*een ei (eieren)*
menu	**la carte**	*een menu*
sugar	**du sucre**	*suiker*
tea	**du thé**	*thee*
wine	**du vin**	*wijn*

...and Read the Menu in French

agneau	lamb	**oie**	goose
bœuf	beef	**petits pois**	peas
canard	duck	**pommes**	apples
champignons	mushrooms	**pommes de terre**	potatoes
chou	cabbage		
choufleur	cauliflower	**porc**	pork
crevettes	shrimps	**poulet**	chicken
épinards	spinach	**pruneaux**	prunes
fraises	strawberries	**raisins**	grapes
haricots verts	green beans	**riz**	rice
jambon	ham	**rognons**	kidneys
lapin	rabbit	**saucisse**	sausage
moules	mussels	**veau**	veal

...and in Dutch

aardappelen	potatoes	*konijn*	rabbit
aardbeien	strawberries	*mosselen*	mussels
bloemkool	cauliflower	*nieren*	kidney
druiven	grapes	*pruimen*	prune
eend	duck	*rodekool*	red cabbage
forel	trout		
frieten (fries)	French fries	*rund*	beef
garnalen	shrimps	*spruitjes*	Brussels sprouts
haas	hare		
kaas	cheese	*tong*	sole
kalfskotelet	veal chop	*uien*	onions
karbonade	chop	*varkensvlees*	pork
kip	chicken	*vis*	fish
		worst	sausage

Enjoying a beer at a pavement café

HANDY TRAVEL TIPS

An A–Z Summary of Practical Information

A

ACCOMMODATION (see also YOUTH HOSTELS and BUDGETING FOR YOUR TRIP)

Brussels has a large number of hotels from which to choose – everything from big, luxurious places to small, budget affairs. The Brussels International Tourist Office publishes a booklet containing information about all the hotels in the greater Brussels area, and includes images of each establishment. The tourist offices in the city can make same-day reservations for you if you arrive without a booking. There is also a central reservations service: BTR (Belgian Tourist Reservations) at boulevard Anspach 111, 1000 Brussels; tel: 02-513 7484; fax: 02-513 9277. (For more information, *see page 130*).

Do you have a single/ double room?	**Avez-vous une chambre pour une/deux personnes?** *Hebt u een eenpersoonskamer/ tweepersoonskamer?*
with bath/shower?	**avec bain/douche** *met een bad/douche*
What's the rate per night?	**Quel est le prix pour une nuit?** *Hoeveel kost het per nacht?*

AIRPORT *(aéroport/luchthaven)*

Brussels National Airport <www.brusselsairport.be> is the major international airport for all of Belgium. It lies 14km (9 miles) northeast of the city. There are frequent connections with other European cities and many cities in the US. For information regarding arrivals and departures, tel: 0900-70000 in Belgium; tel: 32-22-753 7753 from outside the country.

The Airport/City Express railway links the airport with the city centre from 5.30am–11.45pm. Departures are every 15 minutes.

The travelling time is around 25 minutes. These trains stop at the Nord, Centrale and Midi stations of central Brussels, so it's helpful to know which station is nearest to your hotel. Some taxis offer reduced-price return fares – look for a sticker in the corner of the windshield with a white aeroplane on an orange background. Official taxis have blue-and-yellow stickers. Local bus services run from the airport to the suburbs of Brussels, but not to the central area.

Where can I get a taxi?	**Où puis-je trouver un taxi?** *Waar kan ik een taxi nemen?*

How much is it to
    Brussels city centre?
	**Combien coûte la course
	    jusqu'au centre de Bruxelles?**
	*Hoeveel kost het naar het
	    centrum van Brussel?*

Does this bus go to Brussels?	**Ce bus va-t-il à Bruxelles?** *Gaat deze bus naar Brussel?*

B

BICYCLE HIRE *(location de bicyclette/fietsverhuur)*

Brussels and the surrounding countryside are well equipped for cyclists, with special bike lanes. However, the city itself has a number of deceptive gradients and busy, aggressive traffic. Renting a bike is worthwhile for journeys to the Bois de la Cambre and Fôret de Soignes, or out to Tervuren. Pro Vélo offers bicycle hire and guided cycling tours of the city (rue de Londres 15; tel: 02-502 7355; <www.provelo.org>).

I'd like to hire
    a bicycle.
	**J'aimerais louer
	    une bicyclette.**
		*Ik zou graag een
		    fiets huren.*

BUDGETING FOR YOUR TRIP

Brussels can be expensive, but no more than any other major European city. Here are a few sample prices to help with your budgeting. Prices are in euros (€).

Getting to Belgium. The cost of getting to Belgium from the UK and Ireland by air varies enormously. Flying with Ryanair one-way from various airports in both countries to Brussels-Charleroi can cost as little as a few pounds or euros (plus taxes), but £10–30 (€15–45) is probably nearer the average. These rates have forced carriers such as BA, BMI, Virgin Express, Aer Lingus and SN Brussels Airlines to cut their own fares.

Of the other options, going by bus from London is likely to be the cheapest. By train, Eurostar from London to Brussels offers good excursion and advance-purchase deals, as does the Channel Tunnel car-transporter. The cost of going by ferry varies depending on the route, whether travelling as a foot passenger or with a car, and whether a cabin is desired. For a foot passenger, the price varies from about £30 one-way on short crossings to about £100 on long crossings.

Similarly, the cost of transatlantic flights from North America varies greatly (particularly given the uncertainties of post-9/11 and bankruptcies among US carriers). A ticket from a consolidator (bucket-shop), or on a special offer, might still be as low as $500 return.

Accommodation. For a double room with bathroom and breakfast, you can pay less than €50, but for reasonable comfort and facilities, €75–100 is a more realistic starting point; a mid-range hotel will cost €100–250; and expensive hotels begin at €250. What you get varies with the location and the time of year. There's a world of difference in prices between Bruges in high season and the Ardennes in low season.

Eating Out. You can eat well in many Belgian restaurants for less than €25 per person for a three-course meal without wine, but, again, a more reasonable starting point would be around €40–50;

in mid-range establishments, expect to pay €50–75; and in expensive places, above €75.

Car Hire. Expect to pay €60–80 per day for a small car.

Museums. Public museums charge €2.50–5 for adult admission. Privately owned attractions may cost up to €10. Often, there are reduced rates for children, senior citizens and students. The three-day Brussels Card (€30) offers reduced entry prices to many attractions and a public transport pass (see TOURIST INFORMATION).

Public Transport. Tickets for one journey that is interchangeable between buses, trams and metro: €1.40; one-day pass, €3.80; 10-journey ticket €9.80 (see PUBLIC TRANSPORT).

C

CAR HIRE *(location de voitures/autoverhuur)*

With a city centre as compact as that in Brussels, and a well-organised public transport system, there is little need for a car. If you wish to explore the countryside, hiring a vehicle for a couple of days frees you from public transport schedules. All the major car-hire firms are represented in the city.

Your national driver's licence will be accepted, provided you have held it for at least one year. Minimum age limits for hiring vary between 20 and 25 years depending on the company and the size of vehicle you want to hire. Collision Damage Waiver is available, but expensive.

I'd like to rent a car.	**Je voudrais louer une voiture.**
	Ik zou graag een auto huren.
now/tomorrow	**tout de suite/demain**
	nu/morgen
for one day/one week	**pour une journée/une semaine**
	voor een dag/een week

The major international firms can be contacted as follows:
Avis: Brussels National Airport Arrivals Lounge, tel: 02-720 0944, Gare du Midi, 1000 Brussels, tel: 02-527 1705; <www.avis.com>.
Hertz: Brussels National Airport Arrivals Lounge, tel: 02-720 6044, Gare du Midi, 1000 Brussels, tel: 02-524 3100; <www.hertz.com>.
Europcar: Brussels National Airport Arrivals Lounge, tel: 02-721 0592; Gare du Midi, tel: 02-522 9573; <www.europcar.com>.

CLIMATE

Brussels and the west of Belgium have a temperate maritime climate, which means that they generally have warm, wet summers and cool, wet winters.

In summer, there may be as many as seven hours of sunshine per day, with temperatures above 27°C (80°F); however, showers are always a possibility. Winter temperatures drop, but rarely fall below freezing. Rain can be expected just about everyday. You can obtain a current weather forecast by telephoning 0900-27003.

Average daytime temperatures in Brussels:

	J	F	M	A	M	J	J	A	S	O	N	D
°C	5	6	10	13	19	21	23	22	20	14	8	6
°F	41	43	50	55	66	70	74	72	68	57	46	41

CLOTHING

Given the above information about climate, about the only item you will definitely need regardless of the time of year is an umbrella. In summer, the weather can be pleasantly hot, and trousers, T-shirts, shirts and shorts will certainly be useful. However, do not forget to pack a warmer layer, in case there is a cold spell, and a rainproof outer layer. On most evenings you will require a jacket to walk around. In winter, pack warm clothing in addition to a waterproof layer. Don't forget comfortable shoes for sightseeing. Although there are many formally dressed businesspeople, Brussels is a casual city with few dress restrictions. If you intend to visit the theatre, ballet, opera or one of the top restaurants in the city, you should pack something a little more formal, of course. A few restaurants in Brussels do expect a tie and jacket.

CRIME AND SAFETY (see also EMERGENCIES and POLICE)

Brussels is a relatively safe city by European standards, with no serious threat of major crime against visitors. Petty crime can cause problems, and pickpocketing is a threat, particularly during events that attract large numbers of people (such as the jazz festival).

Serious crime is unlikely to be a worry for visitors to Belgium, but it does exist, and is to an extent a growing problem in some cities, including Brussels and Antwerp. Violent offences are rare, but drugs-related muggings and other crimes are increasing. After dark, stay alert if you are in metro and railway stations, or red-light areas; avoid deserted and poorly lit areas and stay out of city centre parks unless there are plenty of other law-abiding people around.

Where's the nearest police station?	**Où est le commissariat de police le plus proche?** *War is het dichtsbijzijnd politiebureau?*
I want to report a theft.	**Je veux porter plainte pour vol.** *Ik wil graag een diefstal melden.*
My handbag/wallet/ passport has been stolen.	**On m'a volé mon sac à main/mon portefeuille/mon passeport.** *Mijn handtas/geldbeurs/ paspoort is gestolen.*
Help! Thief!	**A l'aide! Au voleur!** *Hulp! Dief!*

To minimise the risk of becoming a victim, take a few sensible precautions. Do not carry large amounts of cash or valuables with you. Leave your valuables in the hotel safe. Carry all cash and credit cards in secure pockets. Keep handbags shut and carry them close to your body. Do not leave anything in your hire car, if you have one – petty crime involving vehicles is one of the most common crimes in the city. When walking back to your hotel at night, choose well-lit streets to reach your destination. It's also advisable to park your vehicle in an area that is well lit.

CUSTOMS AND ENTRY REQUIREMENTS

To enter Belgium for stays of up to three months, visitors from European Union (EU) countries need only an identity card, or a passport if your home country has no identity card. Citizens of most other countries, including the US, Canada, Australia, New Zealand and South Africa must be in possession of a valid passport, and in the case of some other countries, of a visa also. Residents of Europe and North America are not subject to health requirements; residents of other countries may be and should check with the local Belgian embassy or consulate before departing for Belgium.

As Belgium belongs to the EU, free exchange of non-duty-free goods for personal use is permitted between Belgium and the UK and Ireland, and other EU countries. There are generous guideline levels of goods for personal use; visitors who bring in or take out greater quantities than these may be required to prove that the excess is for personal use. Residents of non-EU countries may bring

I've nothing to declare.	**Je n'ai rien à déclarer.**
	Ik heb niets aan te geven.
It's for my personal use.	**C'est pour mon usage personnel.**
	Het is voor mijn persoonlijk gebruik.

in 200 cigarettes or 50 cigars or 250g tobacco; 2 litres still wine; 1 litre spirits or 2 litres sparkling or fortified wine; 50g perfume; 0.25 litres eau de toilette.

D

DRIVING (see also CAR HIRE)

To take your car into Belgium, you'll need:

• an international driver's licence or your own driver's licence (held for at least one year)

• car-registration papers

• Green Card (this does not provide cover, but is internationally recognised proof that you have insurance; though not obligatory for EU countries, it's still useful, especially in case of an accident)

• a fire extinguisher and a red warning triangle in case of breakdown

• a national identity sticker for your car

• for right-hand-drive vehicles, headlight adapters to prevent the lights dazzling other drivers

Driving conditions. Drive on the right, and pass on the left. Although you may wish to drive between towns and cities, it is ill-advised to drive within the big cities themselves. Driving is invariably aggressive, and there are complex one-way systems and intersections to negotiate, along with (in some cities) trams, which you are not allowed to overtake and to which you must give way.

Seat belts must be worn by both driver and passengers. The use of dipped headlights is mandatory after dusk and in poor visibility. There are stiff penalties for driving under the influence of alcohol and drugs. Some offences require payment of fines on the spot.

Drivers should normally give way to traffic approaching from the right. A yellow diamond-shaped sign with a white border indicates that drivers on main roads have right of way; if the sign has a diagonal line through it, drivers must give way to traffic from the right.

Motorways. Belgium's motorway *(autoroute/snelweg)* network is excellent, but it and the city ring roads, especially those of Brussels and Antwerp, can get clogged at rush hour. Other main roads are generally free of traffic and weekday travelling is usually smooth. Belgium's accident record, however, is one of the worst in Europe.

Speed limits. On motorways, the limit is 120km/h (75mph); on other main roads it is 90km/h (55mph). In residential areas the speed limit drops to 50km/h (30mph). In all cases, lower limits may be indicated.

Are we on the right road for…?	**Est-ce la bonne route pour…?** *Zijn wij op de juiste weg naar…?*

Parking. There is limited street parking in city centres. Car and coach parks exist in the centres, or in the case of pedestrian-friendly towns such as Bruges, around the perimeter of the centre.

Breakdowns. Belgium's two main motoring organisations are the Touring Club de Belgique and the Royal Automobile Club de Belgique. These have reciprocal arrangements with other national motoring organisations and should be able to help you if you are a member of your own national organisation. In case of breakdown, call Touring Secours/Wegenhulp, tel: 070-344777.

There's been an accident.	**Il y a eu un accident.** *Er is een ongeval gebeurd.*
My car has broken down.	**Ma voiture est en panne.** *Mijn wagen is kapot.*

Fuel and oil: Petrol stations are plentiful, and most international brands of leaded, unleaded and diesel fuel are on sale.

Road signs. International pictographs are in widespread use, but here are some written signs you may encounter:

Arrêtez-vous	*Halt*	Halt
Carrefour	*Kruispunt*	Crossroads
Forte pente	*Gevaarlijke Daling*	Steep hill
Déviation	*Omweg*	Detour
Passage piétons	*Voetganger-* *oversteekplaats*	Pedestrian crossing
Stationnement autorisé	*Parkeren* *Toegelaten*	Parking permitted
Stationnement interdit	*Parkeerverbod*	No parking
Prudence	*Voorzichtig Rijden*	Drive with care
Arrêt de bus	*Bushalte*	Bus stop
Stop	*Stop*	Stop
Sens unique	*Eenrichtingverkeer*	One-way
Danger	*Gevaar*	Danger
Serns interdit	*Verboden Toegang*	No entry
Serrez à droite/ à gauche/	*Rechterhand/* *Linkerhand Houden*	Keep right/left
Impasse	*Doodlopende Weg*	No through road

E

ELECTRICITY

Belgium operates on 220 volts, 50Hz AC, requiring standard two-pin round continental plugs. Visitors should bring – or buy locally – their own adapters, and transformers if needed.

EMBASSIES, CONSULATES AND HIGH COMMISSIONS
(ambassades; consulats/ambassades; consulaten)

Australia: rue Guimard 6–8, 1040 Brussels, tel: 02-286 0500.
Canada: avenue de Tervuren 2, 1040 Brussels, tel: 02-741 0611.
Ireland: rue Wiertz 50, 1040 Brussels, tel: 02-235 6676.
New Zealand: square de Meeûs 1, 1000 Brussels, tel: 02-512 1040.
South Africa: rue de la Loi 26, 1040 Brussels, tel: 02-285 4400.
UK: rue Arlon 85, 1000 Brussels, tel: 02-287 6211.
US: boulevard du Régent 25–7, 1000 Brussels, tel: 02-508 2111.

EMERGENCIES (see also CRIME AND SAFETY and POLICE)

Police	**101**
Ambulance	**100**
Fire	**100**

G

GAY AND LESBIAN TRAVELLERS

For information on Brussels and Wallonia, contact **Infor Homo**, avenue de l'Opale 100, Brussels, tel: 02-733 1024; or the gay and lesbian community centre, **Telsquels**, rue du Marché-au-Charbon 81, Brussels, tel: 02-512 4587. In Flanders, contact the **Federatie Werkgroepen Homoseksualiteit**, Vlaanderenstraat 22, Ghent, tel: 09-238 2626; e-mail: <fwh@innet.be>. The age of consent for gay men is 16.

GETTING THERE

By Air. Many airlines offer direct scheduled flights to Brussels National Airport. SN Brussels Airlines (tel: 070-351313; <www.flysn.com>) is the principal local carrier. British Airways (tel: 0870-850 9850 within the UK for flight information; in Belgium, tel: 02-717 3217; <www.ba.com>) operates flights from several UK airports to Brussels. Flight time from London to Brussels is about one hour. Several smaller airlines operate flights from UK airports to Brussels. They include Virgin Express, BMI and KLM. Aer Lingus (tel: 02-753 2000; <www.aerlingus.ie>) has regular service to Brussels from Dublin and other Irish airports. Ryanair (tel: 0900-10310; <www.ryanair.com>) flies from airports in Britain and Ireland to Charleroi, near Brussels.

American Airlines (tel: 800-433 7300; <www.aa.com>), Delta Airlines (tel: 800-221 1212; <www.delta.com>), and Continental Airlines (tel: 800-525 0280; <www.continental.com>) all offer flights to Brussels. From Canada, Air Canada (tel: 888-247 2262; <www.aircanada.ca>) has services to Brussels.

By Rail. Thalys is a high-speed rail network run by a co-operation of Belgian, Dutch, German and French companies. It operates frequent departures from various northern European cities. For information and reservations in Belgium, tel: 02-528 2828; <www.thalys.com>.

Eurostar operates train services from London (Waterloo Station) through the Channel Tunnel to Brussels. There are frequent departures and the journey time is just over three hours. You must make a reservation. For UK Eurostar information, tel: 0870-160 6600; in Brussels, tel: 02-528 2828; <www.eurostar.com>.

Belgian state railways (SNCB/NMBS) operates local services within Belgium along with international services (tel: 02-528 2828 for details).

By Bus. Eurolines operates bus services between all the major European cities and Brussels (tel: 08705-808080 in the UK, tel: 02-274 1350 in Belgium for bookings; <www.eurolines.com>).

By Boat. There are car ferry crossings daily to Belgium from the UK (Hull to Zeebrugge) with P&O Ferries (tel: 08705-202020 in the UK; tel: 02-710 6444 in Belgium; <www.poferries.com>); and every two days (Rosyth/Edinburgh to Zeebrugge) with Superfast

Ferries (tel: 0870-234 0870 in the UK; tel: 050-252292 in Belgium; <www.superfast.com>).

GUIDES AND TOURS *(guide/gids)*

Brussels has more than 50 guided walking tours (in 14 languages) to help you to make the most of your visit. These are organised by the GBB (Guides Brussels-Belgium), but most programmes do not operate every day. The Discover Brussels walk operates on Saturday and Sunday at 2pm (you must pre-arrange an English tour) from the Brussels International Tourist Office.

Calèche or horse-drawn carriage tours of the city centre take place during the summer. Pick them up at rue Charles Buls (Grand-Place) or make a reservation for up to 18 people (tel: 053-700504).

De Boeck's Sightseeing Tours operates bus tours around the city and beyond with multilingual headset accompaniment. You can book these tours through the Brussels International Tourist Office in the Grand-Place or contact the company directly (tel: 02-513 7744).

H

HEALTH AND MEDICAL CARE

Belgium is a safe destination with no inherent threats to your health. It operates a sophisticated health-care system, and most doctors speak good English.

Medical care is expensive, so do ensure that you have full insurance coverage against any illness or accident. For minor treatments, you may have to pay first and reclaim the payment from your insurance company later. Citizens from other European countries can obtain free medical treatment if they carry an E111 document. This must be completed and certified at a post office before travel.

Most prescription drugs are available in Belgium along with a large range of over-the-counter medications. A pharmacy *(pharmacie/apotheek)*, indicated by a green cross, will employ a qualified member of staff who will be able to advise you about treatments for minor ailments.

The **Cliniques Universitaires St-Luc**, avenue Hippocrate 10; tel: 02-764 1111, has a casualty/emergency department.

Where's the nearest pharmacy?	**Où est la pharmacie la plus proche?** *Waar is de dichtstbijzijnde apotheek?*
I need a doctor/dentist/ a hospital.	**J'ai besoin d'un médecin/ un dentiste/d'aller a l'hôpital.** *Ik heb een arts/tandarts/ ziekenhuis nodig.*

L

LANGUAGE

About 60 percent of Belgians (mostly in the north of the country) speak Dutch (or *Nederlands*, as the language of Flanders and the Netherlands, is called). In Belgium, you will also hear it described as *Vlaans* – Flemish). In Wallonia (southern Belgium), most of the population speaks French. A small percentage of the population of the eastern part of the country speaks German.

Brussels itself is officially bilingual, with most people speaking French. Menus may be printed in English as well as French and Dutch; if they are not, most staff will be able to explain what things are. You will find that many people in tourist situations have some English. The latter is, in fact, widely spoken, with many English-speaking ex-pats living here. But do try using some French or Dutch, it really will be appreciated. The *Berlitz Phrase Book and Dictionary for French* and *The Berlitz Phrase Book and Dictionary for Dutch* cover most situations you are likely to encounter.

Road signs are in the local language of the region. Many Belgian towns have different names in French and Dutch. For instance, Brussels is *Bruxelles* in French and *Brussel* in Dutch; Bruges is *Brugge* in Dutch; Ghent is *Gent* in Dutch and *Gand* in French; Antwerp is *Antwerpen* in Dutch and *Anvers* in French.

LAUNDRY AND DRY CLEANING

Most hotels will do your laundry for a fee, but it is easy to organise your own laundry and dry cleaning while in town. La Comète has a number of outlets in the city. The central office can be found at rue du Noyer 283, 1000 Brussels; tel: 02-773 7002.

M

MAPS

The International Brussels Tourist Office produces a comprehensive map and information booklet of central Brussels. It is ideal for walking tours and costs €3.

MEDIA

Newspapers and magazines. English-language newspapers and magazines are available from railway-station kiosks, larger bookshops and newsstands. Expensive hotels often stock the *International Herald Tribune, Financial Times* and other quality international newspapers. An English-language weekly news and events magazine, *The Bulletin,* is available in Brussels and other large towns.

Have you any English-language newspapers?	**Avez-vous des journaux en anglais?** *Hebt u Engelse kranten?*

Radio and television. The BBC World Service and European-based American networks can be picked up easily. Many hotels have cable television with up to 30 channels, including BBC World, Sky News, CNN International and EuroNews. Belgian and Dutch channels often show English-language films and series in the original language, with local subtitles.

MONEY

The unit of currency in Belgium is the euro (€), divided into 100 cents. Coins in circulation are €2, €1 and 50, 20, 10, 5, 2 and 1 cents. Banknotes are €500, €200, €100, €50, €20, €10 and €5.

Can I pay by credit card?	**Puis-je payer par carte bancaire?** *Mag ik met mijn kredietkaart betalen?*
I want to change some pounds/dollars.	**Je voudrais changer des livres sterling/dollars.** *Ik wil graag een paar pond/ dollar wisselen.*
Can you cash a travellers cheque?	**Changez-vous les chèques de voyage?** *Kan ik geld voor mijn reis cheque krijgen?*
Where's the nearest bank/ currency exchange office?	**Où est la banque/le bureau de change le/la plus proche?** *Waar is de dichtstbijzijnde bank/ het dichtstbijzijnde wisselkantoor?*
Is there a cash machine here?	**Y a-t-il un distributeur de billets?** *Is er hier ergens een geldautomaat?*
How much is that?	**Combien coûte ceci?** *Hoeveel is dat?*

Exchange facilities. Generally, banks offer the best rates, followed by bureaux de change. Bureaux de change can be found at the airport, at each of the Brussels' railway stations and off the Grand-Place, Travellers cheques can be cashed at these locations as long as you have your passport with you. There are currency-exchange machines at Brussels Airport which make transactions in several currencies. Cash machines (ATMs) called 'Bancontact' and 'Mister Cash', which accept non-Belgian cards, are widely available.

Credit cards. Many hotels, restaurants and shops accept payment by international credit cards.

Value-added tax, service charge. A sales (value-added) tax – called TVA in French and BTW in Dutch – is imposed on most goods and services. Hotels, taxi drivers and most restaurants also add a service charge. Both are included in the bill. Some shops operate a tax-refund scheme for non-EU visitors: look for 'Europe Tax-Free Shopping' stickers on the window.

OPENING HOURS

Offices open from 8am or 9am until 5pm or 6pm Mon–Fri.
Banks are open Mon–Fri 9am–4 or 5pm, some on Sat morning.
Shops are generally open from 10am–6pm Mon–Sat, but tourist shops may stay open longer and open on Sun. Department stores are generally open until 8pm on Thurs. There are also a number of night-shops in the city selling a range of food, alcohol and other goods until the early hours of the morning. Post offices are open Mon–Fri, 9am–4pm. The post office at Centre Monnaie is open on Sat morning.
Museums are generally open Tues–Sat 10am–5pm, sometimes closing for one hour at lunchtime between noon and 2pm.

P

POLICE (see also CRIME AND SAFETY and EMERGENCIES)

The police *(police/politie)* can be reached on the emergency **101** telephone number. Officers wear dark-blue uniforms and many of them can speak at least some English. For less urgent police matters, go to **Brussels Central Police Station**, rue du Marché-au-Charbon 30, tel: 02-279 7979, near the Grand-Place.

POST OFFICES *(La Poste/De Poste)*

Belgian postal services are speedy and reliable. The main post office can be found at the Centre Monnaie in place de la Monnaie. Belgian post boxes are red with a stylised bugle in relief on the side.

Postal rates for postcards and letters up to 20g in weight are 45 cents within Europe, and 85 cents for all other destinations. Stamps can be purchased at souvenir shops, newsstands and bookstores.

PUBLIC HOLIDAYS

Belgium's national holidays *(jour férié/openbare feestdag)* are:

1 January	New Year's Day
1 May	Labour Day
21 July	National Day
15 August	Assumption
1 November	All Saints' Day
11 November	Armistice Day (1918)
25 December	Christmas

Movable dates: Easter Monday, Ascension Day, Pentecost Monday.

PUBLIC TRANSPORT

The Société de Transports Intercommunaux Bruxellois (STIB) runs metro, bus and tram services in the metropolitan area of Brussels. With one ticket you can transfer between trams, metro and buses for a period of one hour (you must re-validate your ticket with each change). Tickets can be purchased from STIB offices, metro stations and newsstands. A ticket for one journey is €1.40, and a 10-journey ticket costs €9.80. A one-day pass costs €3.80. These are available from tourist offices in addition to the other sources above. Maps of the network can be obtained from metro offices and tourist offices. Public transport operates from 6am–midnight.

Metro. Metro/subway/underground stations are indicated by a sign with a white M on a blue background. There are information offices at the following stations *(gares)*: Gare du Midi, Brouckère, Rogier and Porte de Namur.

Trams, *pré-métro* and buses. Trams and buses operate on set routes. The *pré-métro* is a section of the tram network in the city centre that operates underground. Red-and-white signs indicate stops for both trams and buses. You must signal the driver to stop if you want to get on. Be aware that some tram stops are located in the middle of the street, with traffic lanes next to them. Although traffic should stop to allow you to board and alight, take care when getting on and off. Be particularly careful if you are travelling with young children.

Where can I get a taxi?	**Où puis-je trouver un taxi?** *Waar kan ik een taxi nemen?*
What's the fare to... ?	**Quel est le prix de la course pour…?** *Hoeveel kost een rit naar…?*

When's the next bus/
    train to...?
	**A quelle heure est le prochain bus/
	    train pour…?**
	 *Wanneer is de volgende bus/
	    trein naar…?*

I want a ticket to...	**Je voudrais un billet pour…** *Ik wil graag een kaart naar…*
single/return	**aller-simple/aller-retour** *enkele reis/retour* (also known as **un direct**/*een direkt*)

Taxis. There are many taxis operating in the city centre. Basic fares start at €2.35 (€4.21 at night), then €1.14 per km (0.6 mile) within the greater Brussels area. To contact Taxis Bleus to make a booking, tel: 02-268 0000.

Trains. For Travel within Belgium (to Antwerp, Bruges and Ghent) Belgian state railways (SNCB/NMBS) operates services. Excursion tickets include the cost of transport and the entrance fee for an attraction in certain areas, and may save you money. Tel: 02-528 2828 for details.

Buses. The bus is not as quick as the train, but perhaps it is more scenic. Walloon Brabant (mostly destinations south of Brussels) services are operated by TEC, tel: 010-235353; Flemish Brabant (mostly destinations north of Brussels) services are operated by De Lijn; tel: 070-220200 for information.

R

RELIGION

Belgium is a predominantly Catholic country, but there are a number of Protestant churches. In Brussels, it is possible to attend English-language services. There are also mosques and synagogues, which hold regular meetings. For further details on services, contact Brussels-Accueil on tel: 02-511 8178.

T

TELEPHONES

When making international calls, dial 00 followed by the country code: Belgium 32; UK 44; USA and Canada 1; Ireland 353; Australia 61; New Zealand 64, South Africa 27. Most hotels allow direct di-alling for international calls, but this can be expensive. Contact an international telephone company to route your call. AT&T has a network of numbers for this purpose. The call is charged to your credit card.

To call another Belgian number inside Belgium, you always need to dial the full area code, even when you are calling a number from within the same area. Some area codes are: Brussels 02, Antwerp 03, Bruges 050, Ghent 09.

Call boxes can be found in all public places in Brussels; those permitting international direct-dial calls show European flags. Machines accept 10 cents, 20 cents, 50 cents and €1 coins and phone cards *(telecards/telekaarten)*. Phone cards can be purchased in grocery stores, from newsstands, and at post offices and railway stations. Rates for telephone calls are listed in phone kiosks.

TIME ZONES

Belgium is in the Central European Time zone, which is Greenwich Mean Time (GMT) plus one hour in winter and two hours in summer (between the end of March and the end of October, clocks are advanced one hour). Belgium is one hour ahead of the UK and Ireland, six hours ahead of US Eastern Standard Time, and 10 hours behind Australia (Sydney).

New York	London	**Belgium**	Jo'burg	Sydney	Auckland
6am	11am	**noon**	1pm	10pm	midnight

TIPPING

Service is included in most bills, so tipping is not necessary. Nevertheless, tips are still appreciated (though not always expected) by some service personnel, particularly in places that cater to a large number of tourists. To tip as Belgians do (when they do at all) in restaurants, round up your bill to the nearest convenient amount or leave about 5 percent. A tip of 10 percent would be considered generous in most cases.

Service is also included in taxi fare rates, so any extra tip is completely at your discretion.

TOILETS

There are public toilets in all metro and railway stations, and in shopping malls (such as Anspach, Centre de Monnaie). In many public toilets, 'tipping' the attendant about 25–50 cents (or whatever minimum amount is posted) is mandatory. In small cafés and restaurants, men's and women's toilets may be only notionally separated.

Where are the toilets?	**Où sont les toilettes?**
	Waar is het WC, alstublieft?

TOURIST INFORMATION

Brussels has its own tourist information office, which produces a number of maps and information guides to help you on your trip. There is a small charge for some items. It also issues a Brussels Card, valid for three days, with reductions on the entry prices of numerous attractions throughout the city and a public transport pass (€30). Contact them at:

Brussels International Tourism, Town Hall (Hôtel de Ville), Grand-Place, 1000 Brussels, tel: 02-513 8940, fax: 02-513 8320, <www.brusselsinternational.be>. There is also an information office at the arrivals lounge of Brussels National Airport, and another in the TGV/Thalys/Eurostar hall at Gare du Midi.

The **Belgian National Tourist Office** has international offices:
UK: (Brussels and Wallonia): 217 Marsh Wall, London E14 9FJ, tel: 0906-302 0245, brochure line: 0800-954 5245, fax: 020-7531 0393, <www.belgiumtheplaceto.be>. (Brussels and Flanders): 1a Cavendish Square, London W1G 0LD, tel: 0906-302 0245, brochure line: 0800-954 5245, fax: 020-7307 7731, <www.visitflanders.co.uk>.
US: 220 East 42nd Street, Suite 3402, New York, NY 10017, tel: 212-758 8130, fax: 212-355 7675, <www.visitbelgium.com>.
Canada: English-speaking residents can contact the New York office (*see above*, and by calling tel: 514-457 2888). For French-

speaking residents: Office de Promotion de Tourisme Wallonie-Bruxelles, 43 rue de Buade, Bureau 525, Quebec Ville, Quebec G1R 4A2, tel: 0877-792 4939 or 418-692 4939, fax: 418-692 4974, <www.visitbelgium.com>.

Brussels: Belgian National Tourist Office, rue du Marché-aux-Herbes 63, 1000 Brussels, tel: 02-504 0390, fax: 02-504 0270, <www.belgium.opt.be> or <www.visitflanders.com>.

Where is the tourist office?	**Où est l'office du tourisme?**	*Waar is het verkeers bureau?*

W

WEBSITES

Here are some websites to help you plan your trip: <www.belgiquetourisme.net>; <www.visitbelgium.com>; <www.belgiumtheplaceto.be>; <www.brusselsinternational.be>; <www.visitflanders.co.uk>; <www.visitantwerpen.be>; <www.bruges.be>; <www.ghent.be>.

Y

YOUTH HOSTELS *(auberge de jeunesse/jeugdherberg)*

There are a number of good youth hostels in the city, including three within the central Brussels area (the zip 1000 area). It is important to make a booking especially at peak times to ensure that you get a bed.

Auberge de Jeunesse Jacques Brel, rue de la Sablonnière 30, tel: 02-218 0187, fax: 02-217 2005, <www.laj.be>. This hostel also has facilities for disabled travellers.

Jeugdherberg Breughel, rue du St-Esprit 2, tel: 02-511 0436, fax: 02-512 0711, <www.jeugdherbergen.be>.

Sleep Well, rue du Damier 23, tel: 02-218 5050, fax: 02-218 1313, <www.sleepwell.be>.

Recommended Hotels

Brussels has a large number of hotels ranging from the large and luxurious to the small and simple. Though many hotels rate themselves by the international star system, there is no definitive standard. The national star rating is not necessarily an indication of the style and standard of a hotel, but simply a confirmation that it has certain facilities.

High season comes in the summer months (May–September), with low season in winter (November–March). However, there are rises in demand when large conventions are in town or special events such as the Jazz Marathon take place. Prices are generally lower in winter, though some hotels catering predominantly to business clients offer good discounts for weekend stays throughout the year, as this is when they have spare capacity.

The prices below indicate room rates per night for a double room. Most budget and moderately priced hotels include breakfast in the room rate, but many expensive hotels do not. Older hotels tend not to have wheelchair access, although newer hotels generally have ramps. Please contact an establishment directly if this is a specific requirement. To telephone from abroad, dial 0032, followed by one of the numbers listed below (minus the initial 0 of the area code).

€€€€	over 400 euros
€€€	250–400 euros
€€	100–250 euros
€	under 100 euros

BRUSSELS

L'Amigo €€€€ *rue de l'Amigo 1–3, 1000 Brussels; tel: 02-547 4747; fax: 02-502 2805; <www.roccofortehotels.com>*. One of the most elegant hotels in the city and situated just off the Grand-Place, the Amigo makes a relaxing place in which to retreat after a day of sightseeing. Facilities include a restaurant and bar. Breakfast is not included. 178 rooms.

Astoria €€€ *rue Royale 103, 1000 Brussels; tel: 02-227 0505; fax: 02-217 1150; <www.sofitel.com>*. This beautiful period hotel has fine public rooms with stained glass and chandeliers. The bedrooms are also in period style, with painted wood panelling. Enjoy the luxury of days gone by, only with the added comfort of modern amenities. Facilities include a restaurant, bar and fitness room. Breakfast is not included. 118 rooms.

Astrid Centre €€ *place du Samedi 11, 1000 Brussels; tel: 02-219 3119; fax: 02-219 3170; <www.astridhotel.be>*. Modern hotel near St Catherine's Church. The rooms have Scandinavian furnishings. Facilities include a restaurant and bar. Breakfast is included. Access for disabled guests. 100 rooms.

Barsey Mayfair €€€€ *avenue Louise 381–83, 1050 Brussels; tel: 02-649 9800; fax: 02-640 1764; <www.hyatt.com>*. A luxury hotel situated near the historic city centre and only minutes away from the best designer shopping in Brussels (on avenue Louise). The Barsey Mayfair has well-furnished rooms, a bar and friendly helpful staff. Breakfast is not included. 99 rooms.

Bedford €€–€€€ *rue du Midi 135, 1000 Brussels; tel: 02-507 0000; fax: 02-507 0010; <www.hotelbedford.be>*. The Bedford is close to the Gare du Midi. The décor in the rooms is a little unimaginative, and rooms also vary greatly in terms of natural light and noise levels. Facilities include a restaurant, bar and shops. Breakfast is included. 309 rooms.

Les Bluets € *rue Berckmans 124, 1060 Brussels; tel: 02-534 3983; fax: 02 543 0970; <www.belge.net/bluets>*. In a townhouse dating from 1864 off avenue Louise, this small, quirky – and non-smoking – hotel, filled with antiques, is full of country-house charm. The feeling of staying at a rural residence extends into the rooms, which are old-fashioned and comfortable rather than modern and efficient. Breakfast is included. 10 rooms.

Comfort Art Hotel Siru €€ *place Rogier 1, 1000 Brussels; tel: 02-203 3580; fax: 02-203 3303; <www.comforthotelsiru.com>*.

Situated on a redeveloped square near the Gare du Nord, the Siru is a comfortable hotel with a difference. More than 100 contemporary artists, including painters, sculptors and comic-strip draughtsmen, have been allowed to decorate the rooms and public areas, so each space makes an individual statement. Facilities include a restaurant and bar. Breakfast is included. 101 rooms.

Conrad Brussels €€€€ *avenue Louise 71, 1050 Brussels; tel: 02-542 4242; fax: 02-542 4200; <www.conradhotels.com>.* Large and sprawling, this business-oriented hotel on Brussels' classiest avenue is among the most expensive in town. You get what you pay for, including oceans of white marble, a heated indoor pool, a health club and spa, and a refined French restaurant. There can be few in-room amenities the Conrad has neglected to install in its 269 luxuriously furnished rooms. Breakfast is extra.

Le Dixseptième €€ *rue de la Madeleine 25, 1000 Brussels; tel: 02-517 1717; fax: 02-502 6424; <www.ledixseptieme.be>.* This intimate hotel is just across from the Galeries Royales St-Hubert, so it's very central. The house was home to the Spanish ambassador in the 18th century, and retains much of its grandeur. Today, it's a small hotel offering a different kind of upmarket accommodation, with antique furniture and wood floors. Facilities include a garden and bar. Breakfast is included. 24 rooms.

Floris Grand-Place €€ *rue des Harengs 6–8, 1000 Brussels; tel: 02-514 0760; fax: 02-548 9039; <www.grouptorus.com>.* Many rooms in this small hotel, situated in a historic district and street leading off the Grand-Place, have beams and little windows. They are nicely furnished, but the bathrooms are small. You can't beat the location for both sightseeing and eating out. Breakfast is included. 11 rooms.

George V € *rue t'Kint 23, 1000 Brussels; tel: 02-513 5093; fax: 02-513 4493; <www.george5.com>.* Small, family-run hotel situated five minutes west of the Bourse in a residential area. Rooms are basic, but nicely furnished. Breakfast is included. Private parking. 16 rooms.

Hotel du Congrès €€ *rue du Congrès 42, 1000 Brussels; tel: 02-217 1890; fax: 02-217 1897; <www.hotelducongres.com>*. This hotel, formerly two private houses, is just off rue Royale, 10 minutes from the Grand-Place. It's a clean, basic option with a generous breakfast included. 52 rooms.

Métropole €€€–€€€€ *place de Brouckère 31, 1000 Brussels; tel: 02-217 2300; fax: 02-218 0220; <www.metropolehotel.be>*. The grande-dame of Brussels' hotels, the Métropole is sumptuous, with fantastic marble decorations, although some areas are showing their age. Enjoy a drink at the street terrace café even if you don't book a room–it's the place to be seen. Facilities include a restaurant, bar, fitness room and beauty therapy centre. Breakfast is extra. 410 rooms.

Montgomery €€€€ *avenue Tervuren 134, 1150 Brussels; tel: 02-741 8511; fax: 02-741 8500; <www.montgomery.be>*. Situated near the Parc Cinquantenaire, the Montgomery aims to offer an English country-house atmosphere in the city. The library has volumes in several languages, and other facilities include a restaurant, bar, comprehensive fitness room and sauna. Breakfast is not included. 61 rooms.

Mozart € *rue du Marché-aux-Fromages 23, 1000 Brussels; tel: 02-502 6661; fax: 02-502 7758; <www. hotel-mozart.be>*. Situated one street behind the Grand-Place in the heart of a restaurant and bar area, the Mozart offers a good budget option to those who want to be very central. Rooms have antique furnishings and old paintings. Breakfast is not included. 47 rooms.

Le Plaza €€€–€€€€ *boulevard Adolphe Max 118–26, 1000 Brussels; tel: 02-278 0100; fax: 02-278 0101; <www.leplaza-brussels.be>*. Situated just a short stroll from place de Brouckère, Le Plaza was a major attraction for visitors during the 1930s and 1940s, but it passed a number of years in the doldrums before being totally refurbished in fine style in the late 1990s. Unfortunately, its girly-bar neighbours are not quite so salubrious. Le Plaza's facilities include a bar, restaurant, sauna and fitness room. Breakfast is extra. 193 rooms.

Sabina € *rue du Nord 78, 1000 Brussels; tel: 02-218 2637; fax: 02-219 3239; <www.hotelsabina.be>*. In a street off rue Royale, this small hotel in a well-maintained 19th-century townhouse features some of the attributes of a private residence. The rooms don't quite match the warmth and homeliness of the public spaces, but are quiet and tastefully modern, and some have kitchenettes. Breakfast is included. 24 rooms.

Ustel €€ *square de l'Aviation 6–8, 1070 Brussels; tel: 02-520 6053; fax: 02-520 3328; <www.grouptorus.com>*. Friendly three-star hotel just minutes from the Gare du Midi. There is a lively bar with a large terrace, and an excellent restaurant sits next door in the old historic flood-lock building of the River Senne. Rooms with kitchenettes are available for longer stays. Breakfast is included. 100 rooms.

Welcome €–€€ *Quai au Bois-à-Brûler 23, 1000 Brussels; tel: 02-219 9546; fax: 02-217 1887; <www.hotelwelcome.com>*. This small hotel, in a townhouse dating from 1896 at the Marché-aux-Poissons, makes up in personal attention for what it lacks in size. Each room is individually styled on a different national theme, with antiques and ethnic fittings. There's no shortage of good seafood restaurants just outside on the Fish Market. Breakfast is included. 15 rooms.

ANTWERP

De Witte Lelie €€€ *Keizerstraat 16, 2000 Antwerp; tel: 03-226 1966; fax: 03-234 0019; <www.dewittelelie.be>*. Magnificent suites-only hotel just minutes away from Grote Markt and other attractions in central Antwerp. The courtyard is a peaceful retreat from the bustle of the city. Facilities include a restaurant and bar, and breakfast is included. 10 rooms.

Rubenshof € *Amerikalei 115–17, 2000 Antwerp, tel: 03-237 0789; fax: 03-248 25 94; <www.rubenshof.be>*. Near the Royal Museum of Fine Arts, this small family hotel used to be the residence of Belgium's cardinal and features lavishly appointed public spaces. The rooms are plain, but comfortable. 22 rooms.

BRUGES

Dante €€ *Coupure 29, 8000 Bruges; tel: 050-340194; fax: 050-345539; <www.hoteldante.be>.* A 10-minute walk from the historic centre, this quiet, canalside hotel offers modern yet comfortable accommodation. There is a restaurant and bar, and breakfast is included. 22 rooms.

Hans Memling €–€€ *Kuiperstraat 18, 8000 Bruges; tel: 050-471212; fax: 050-471210; <www.grouptorus.com>.* A small hotel situated in the heart of the city, the Hans Memling is perfect for exploring this historic town. Pleasant breakfast room (breakfast is included). There is a bar. 36 rooms.

De Orangerie €€€ *Kartuizerinnenstraat 10, 8000 Bruges; tel: 050-341649; fax: 050-333016; <www.hotelorangerie.com>.* An attractive 17th-century canal house set opposite the Dijver, this hotel is in an ideal location. The rooms are individually designed and furnished to luxurious standards. There is a bar, and guests have the use of the sauna and pool of the Tuilerieen Hotel (a sister hotel) on the opposite side of the road. Breakfast is included. 19 rooms.

GHENT

Novotel Gent-Centrum €€€ *Goudenleeuwplein 5, 9000 Ghent; tel: 09-224 2230; fax: 09-224 3295; <www.novotel.com>.* Part of the European Novotel chain of hotels, this is probably one of its most attractive. Situated in the centre of Ghent, it incorporates a 14th-century crypt. Facilities include a restaurant, bar and pool. Breakfast is not included. 117 rooms.

Sofitel Gent-Belfort €€€€ *Hoogpoort 63, 9000 Ghent; tel: 09-233 3331; fax: 09-233 1102; <www.sofitel.com>.* Situated opposite the Stadhuis (Town Hall), the Sofitel is centrally located and in a perfect position for exploring the town. Facilities include a restaurant, bar, fitness room and sauna. Breakfast is extra. 127 rooms.

Recommended Restaurants

In most of the finer restaurants listed below, it is best to make a reservation; for a few of them, you will need to book weeks in advance or hope for a last-minute cancellation.

Keep in mind that many restaurants accept dogs in the dining room and on outside terraces. Smoking is still popular in Belgium, including in bars and restaurants, although, in summer, many restaurants have outside dining, which alleviates the problem. The following prices are for dinner for one person without wine. If you want to make a reservation from outside Belgium, dial 0032 and one of the numbers listed below (minus the initial 0 of the area code).

€€€€	over 100 euros
€€€	60–100 euros
€€	30–60 euros
€	under 30 euros

BRUSSELS

GRAND-PLACE/FISH MARKET/ILOT SACRÉ

La Belle Maraîchère €€ *place Ste-Catherine 11; tel: 02-512 9759.* Seafood delivered fresh from the coast is the speciality at this restaurant. It is served in a range of dishes. The fishermen's stew is delicious. Open daily except Wed, lunch noon–2.30pm, dinner 6pm–10pm.

Chez Léon € *rue des Bouchers 14–24; tel: 02-511 1415.* Mussels are big in Belgium, both literally and figuratively, and nowhere more so than at this mussels specialist near the Grand-Place – something that has been the case since 1893. It's not fancy, and the approach even verges on fast-food, but there's nothing wrong with its mollusc speciality, served in a variety of ways, the most basic of which is *marinières* (steamed in a vegetable stock).

Comme Chez Soi €€€€ *place Rouppe 22; tel: 02-512 2921.* Pierre Wynants, the proprietor of this restaurant with three Michelin stars, is one of the world's most creative chefs. The restaurant is styled in early-20th-century Art Nouveau style in homage to Victor Horta. The dishes use the best of local ingredients – a delight for the senses. You can eat in the dining room or take one of the tables in the kitchen. Book as early as possible or try for a last minute cancellation. Jacket and tie required. Open lunch noon–2pm, dinner 7pm–10pm. Closed Mon, Tues, national holidays and all of July.

L'Ecailler du Palais Royal €€€ *rue Bodenbroeck 18; tel: 02-512 8715.* This restaurant offers a gastronomic event featuring exquisite seafood, fine wine and impeccable service. The *plat du jour* is a great budget option at lunchtime. Open lunch noon–2.30pm, dinner 7pm–10.30pm. Closed Sun, national holidays and Aug.

In 't Spinnekopke €€ *place du Jardin-aux-Fleurs 1; tel: 02-511 8695.* Said to be the oldest tavern in Brussels, In 't Spinnekopke serves ample portions of Flemish dishes accompanied by a choice of more than 100 Belgian beers. You'll find it just beyond place St-Géry. Open Mon–Fri, lunch noon–3pm, dinner 6pm–11pm; Sat dinner only.

't Kelderke €–€€ *Grand-Place 15; tel: 02-513 7344.* A typical Brussels bar/restaurant hidden away in a cellar room below the Grand-Place. It serve the very best Flemish dishes, all washed down with excellent beer. The place has an informal atmosphere and is always noisy and very busy because it's such good value. It could be too smoky for some, though. Open daily noon–2am.

La Maison du Cygne €€€ *rue Charles-Buls 2; tel: 02-511 8244.* Originally home of the butcher's guild before becoming a tavern frequented by Marx and Engels, this place is now one of the best restaurants in town, specialising in French dishes. In additional to the delicious food, the ornate dining room on the second floor has great views over the Grand-Place. Open Mon–Fri, lunch 11am–3pm, dinner 7.15pm–10pm; Sat dinner only. Closed during Aug.

La Manufacture €€ *rue Notre-Dame du Sommeil 12–20; tel: 02-502 2525.* A beacon of good taste in a former designer leather-goods factory, in an unprepossessing neighbourhood. You dine on French-based world cuisine, amid iron pillars and exposed air ducts in the refurbished workshop; for the décor, think wood floors, leather benches, polished wood and stone tables. On sunny summer days, the shaded outdoor terrace is a pleasant place to eat.

La Moulière €€ *4 place Ste-Catherine 23; tel: 02-219 6549.* The place to come for that Belgian favourite: mussels. That's all they sell here, served in just about every way you could imagine. Open: winter, lunch Mon–Fri 11.30am–2pm; dinner Mon–Sat 6.30pm–9.30pm; summer, lunch Tues–Fri 11.30am–2pm; dinner daily 6.30pm–9.30pm.

De l'Ogenblik €€ *4 galerie des Princes; tel: 02-511 6151.* On the edge of the Galeries Royales St-Hubert, this restaurant combines the simple décor of a chic French brasserie with Belgian service and a Franco-Belgian menu of meat and seafood dishes. Open Mon–Sat, lunch noon–2.30pm, dinner 7pm–midnight.

La Roue d'Or 26 €€ *rue des Chapeliers 26; tel: 02-514 2554.* This Art Deco brasserie has murals inspired by Magritte. If you can manage to keep your appetite in the profusion of silver gilt, you'll enjoy a typical Belgian menu with a few French dishes. Open daily noon–12.30am.

LE SABLON/LES MAROLLES

Bleu de Toi €€€ *rue des Alexiens 73; tel: 02-502 4371.* Pretty restaurant on a street just west of the church of Notre Dame de la Chapelle. There are three small intimate dining areas, including a vine-covered terrace. The menu is based on French cuisine with modern twists. Open lunch noon–2pm, dinner 7.30pm–11.30pm, closed Sat lunch and all day Sun.

La Canne à Sucre €€ *rue des Pigeons 12; tel: 02-513 0372.* Come here for cuisine from the French Antilles–Martinique. Boudin sausage, *court bouillon* piquant sauces and conch stew are all specialities worth trying. You will also find splendid Martinique rum. Open Tues–Sat, dinner only 7.30pm–midnight. Closed the week of 21 July.

La Grande Porte €€–€€€ *rue Notre Seigneur 9; tel: 02-512 8998.* Very informal eatery with friendly staff. The Belgian dishes are delicious and come in enormous portions, so bring your appetite. Good range of beers and reasonable house wine. Open lunch noon–2.30pm, dinner 7pm–1am. Closed Sat lunch and all day Sun.

Au Stekerlapatte €€ *rue des Prêtres 4; tel: 02-512 8681.* Brussels roast chicken and pig's feet are two of the specialities in this brasserie behind the Palais du Justice. A local favourite. Open Wed–Sun, dinner 7pm–1am.

Trente Rue de la Paille €€–€€€ *rue de la Paille 30; tel: 02-512 0715.* Just south of place du Grand-Sablon, this restaurant has an interesting menu, which mixes different meats or fish within one dish. Good wine list. Open Mon–Sat, lunch noon–2.30pm, dinner 7pm–11.30pm. Closed 15 July–15 Aug and national holidays.

BEYOND THE OLD CITY

Bruneau €€€€ *avenue Broustin 75; tel: 02-427 6978.* A little way from the centre, near the National Basilica, Bruneau is one of the best restaurants in town and has a faithful following. Contemporary gastronomic menu. Open Mon–Thurs, lunch noon–2.30pm, dinner 7pm–10pm, closed Tues evening.

Le Chalet de la Forêt €€€ *drève de Lorraine 43; tel: 02-374 5416.* Fine French cuisine is served in the elegant dining room or on the terrace. Le Chalet is situated at the edge of the Forêt de Soignes, making it a perfect lunch venue on your tours to Waterloo or Tervuren. Open Mon–Fri, lunch noon–2.30pm, dinner 7pm–9pm.

La Grand Ecluse €€–€€€ *boulevard Poincaré 77; tel: 02-522 3025.* Just across the *petite ceinture*, this restaurant was once a lock house for the river and canal system, and the beautifully renovated lock mechanism adds to the innovative overall design. Terrace at the rear. The excellent food is based on French cuisine. Open daily, lunch noon–2.30pm, dinner 7–10pm.

La Quincaillerie €€–€€€ *rue du Page 45; tel 02-538 2553.* Situated near the Musée Horta, this restaurant is housed in a late-19th-century warehouse. The industrial feel has been kept in the truly splendid décor, and the whole place hums with chatter. A typical brasserie with a twist. Belgian and continental dishes are on the menu here. Open lunch Mon–Fri noon–2.30pm, dinner daily 7pm–midnight.

De Ultieme Hallucinatie €€–€€€ *rue Royale 316; tel: 02-217 0614.* Near Le Botanique, this brasserie is famed for its Art Nouveau interior, created in 1904. There is a restaurant with a French haute cuisine menu for formal service, and a brasserie for quick, less-formal service. Restaurant open Mon–Fri lunch noon–2.30pm, dinner 7pm–10.30pm; Sat dinner only. Brasserie open Mon–Fri 11am–2.30am, Sat and Sun 3pm–2am.

ANTWERP

't Fornuis €€€€ *Reyndersstraat 24; tel: 03-233 6270.* Excellent French cuisine served in this traditional brick house near to the Musée Plantin-Moretus. Open Mon–Fri, lunch noon–3pm, dinner 7pm–1pm.

Rooden Hoed €€ *Oude Koornmarkt 25, tel: 03-233 28 44.* Reputed to be Antwerp's oldest restaurant, this 250-year-old establishment situated near the cathedral provides hearty quantities of regional Belgian and French dishes, some of them old standbys and some modern.

Sir Anthony Van Dijck €€–€€€ *Oude Koornmarkt 16, tel: 03-231 6170.* Occupying a superb location in the restored 16th-century Vlaeykensgang courtyard, this modern French-Flemish restaurant is a labour of love for its owner/chef, who removed himself from Michelin-star stress to do something that was considerably more to his liking. The result is a relaxed experience and truly memorable cuisine.

BRUGES

Breydel-De Coninck €–€€ *Breidelstraat 24; tel: 050-339746.* Situated in the street that connects the Burg and the Markt, this long-standing exponent of the Belgian obsession with mussels has traditional style and wood-beamed ceilings. It serves the multifaceted mollusc in a variety of ways – the most popular of which is the basic, big steaming potful – and all are worth going back for. Other seafood dishes, such as lobster and eels, are on the menu too.

Spinola €€€€ *Spinolarei 1; tel: 050-341785.* Traditional Flemish tapestries adorn the dining room of this, one of the best restaurants in town, just off Jan van Eyckplein. Fish dishes are a speciality. Open Tues–Sun, lunch noon–2pm, dinner 7pm–10pm. Closed Mon.

GHENT

Belga Queen €€–€€€ *Graslei 10; tel: 09-280 0100.* This beautiful gabled guild house features both a bar (on the second floor) and a restaurant (third floor). Stone walls and a vaulted ceiling give the rooms a cosy and inviting atmosphere. Tables by the window have wonderful views over the canal. Serves traditional Flemish cuisine. Open daily, bar from 11am, restaurant noon–2pm, dinner 7–10pm.

Keizershof €€ *Vrijdagmarkt 47; tel: 09-223 4466.* Situated on Ghent's lively market square, this large, rambling restaurant has enough space that even when it's full it doesn't seem crowded. Diners pile into hearty portions of Belgian and continental food, amid a décor of wooden ceiling beams, plain wood tables and fashionably tattered walls. In summer, there's outdoor eating in the courtyard.

INDEX